LAKELAND TOWNS AND VILLAGES

MARDALE
twin town
with
Atlantis

COLIN SHELBOURN
Photographs by David Jones

published & edited by Hunter Davies
author of 'The Good Guide to the Lakes

Lakeland Towns and Villages by Colin Shelbourn
Photographs by David Jones
Edited and Introduction by Hunter Davies

First published in Great Britain, 1988,
by Forster Davies Ltd., Loweswater and London.

Typeset by Cardtoons Publications Ltd., Windermere, Cumbria.
Printed and bound in Cumbria by Titus Wilson & Sons Ltd.,
Stricklandgate, Kendal.
Distributed by Century Hutchinson, 62-65 Chandos Place, London,
WC2. All trade orders to Tiptree Book Services, Tiptree, Essex, CD5 0SR.
Tel: 0621-816362.

ISBN 0 9509 190 5 5

Cover photographs: Boot and Cockermouth

To N.E.S.

Acknowledgements

My thanks to everyone who suffered being badgered for opinions for
the appendix and to Michael Moon, for abundant information on
Whitehaven. Pam Grant for putting up with the Great Computer Hunt.
Also my sister, Lorna, who didn't help at all with this book, but has
threatened to take me out rock climbing if she doesn't get a mention. Ron
Palmer, of Titus Wilsons Ltd., provided invaluable help in getting the
book into print. And finally, Paul and Rick Fry of Lakeland Computer
Services, Ambleside, for introducing me to the world of the Apple
Macintosh and smoothing over any minor problΣμxxms along the
way.

Contents

Another busy Bank Holiday in Windermere

Introduction

In our minds, we've been calling this "Urban Lakeland", but it doesn't quite go, doesn't quite sound pretty enough, doesn't quite encourage you to rush out and buy buy buy. And yet it's been our intention from the beginning to look at non-rural Lakeland, the towns and the villages, so it's been an easy way of lumping them together. The trouble with 'urban' is that you immediately think of some massive metropolitan sprawl, like London or Manchester, or some mini metropolitan sprawl, like say, well, Barrow. No one wants to think of them, shudder, shudder, when you're wandering lonely as a daffodil in the heart of the Lakes, Nature's nicest gift to the British Isles.

We will always be grateful to the Blessed Wainwright for what he did for the fells, with those seven wonderful books, so idiosyncratic, so personal, yet comprehensive and totally invaluable. (Let's not talk about his later commercial coffee table books.) It's scarcely believable that no one had done such a piece of work before, such a piece of worshipping, certainly not the way he did it. We've had over 200 years of Lakeland books, but he was the first to produce a personal guide, in words and drawings, to every fell.

The mountains have also been well covered over the centuries. There's no single mountain book which stands above the pack, but there have been some first class ones, for the specialist climbers and the gentler toiler. Lakeland walks generally are more than well catered for, though I suspect some plagiarising is now taking place, with walks being lifted, rather than trodden, as yet another London publisher, pushing out yet another series of Countryside books, needs his instant Lakeland guide and says quick, let's shove in ten walks.

The tarns of Lakeland have their masterpiece, that beautifully illustrated book by W. Heaton Cooper, though it will cost you. As for the general books, a guide which attempts to consider everything in Lakeland, then of course there is one which is head and shoulders above the field, and what a bargain, what a little gem. I refer of course to *The Good Guide to the Lakes* . Make sure you have the latest edition.

It seemed, however, that the Towns and Villages and Hamlets had been neglected. There is a feeling that you come to the Lakes purely for, well, the Lakes. True. Plus the mountains, fells and all that natural stuff. The idea is to get out, breath in, shake it all about, do the hokey cokey up to the top of Skiddaw with all the other orange anoraks, then feel really good. It's not done in certain quarters to rave about the Manmade masterpieces, the artificial attractions, but you will be missing some of the treasures of Lakeland if you don't take in the farmhouses, note the strange slates and the stone work, admire the stately homes which, yes,

Lakeland does have, or enjoy the small towns such as Hawkshead, or even the bigger ones, such as Keswick and Windermere. Even on a crowded day, they have areas and facilities which should be seen. And if it is a crowded day, there are emptier towns, just away from the centre, which are pure delight, such as Cockermouth.

We might deny it, but in fact most Lakeland visitors and residents spend a huge amount of time in the towns and villages. And not all of it is just trying to park. It's where we stay, eat, shop, gape, shelter, drink, dry out, get entertained, get educated, retreat to in poor weather, return to after good weather. There are some folk, tut tut, who in poor weather and in good weather never seem to leave the towns, but throng the pavements, looking for slate table lamps. Someone must buy them.

We decided that of the thirteen million annual visitors to the Lakes, about 12.9 million of them could do with some good, opinionated, information, just on the towns and villages. Colin Shelbourn was going to do everything in his own fair hand at first, a Lakeland Wainwright, without an ounce of printer's type, and he has a terribly neat hand, as all readers of *The Westmorland Gazette* will know, but he suddenly went all modern and technological. Not just a computer and word processor, wow, he has his own typesetting thingy. (Fill in the gap, Col. I dunno what it's called. Oh, it's an Apple Macintosh. Thanks.) So this book has been brought to you direct from his own little fingers. The maps are also his, but done in the old fashioned method, sucking a pencil.

I decided against colour photies. Call me mean, okay I am mean, but you see the same yummy unbelievably garish, chocolate box, colour calendar stuff everywhere. (That's what most of those London publishers put their money into, not the words or the research.) I've always been a fan of those old Abraham postcards. Not just because they reproduce so well, and they're so old you don't have to pay copyright, but because I honestly think they were brilliant. No one seems to do those sort of studied black and white photos today, least of all of urban scenes. Lakeland is now full of amateur snappers. Many give up their work, their homes, to come here and capture Friar's Crag at sunset, or morning at Tarn Hows. As if no one has ever thought of it before.

So we had a county wide competition for black and white pictures, of towns and villages. About fifty people entered, and we whittled it down to a short list of three, before choosing, taran ta ta, David Jones from Grange-over-Sands. We rather rushed him, I'm afraid, but then publishers do that, while real artists want to take their time and photograph for ever.

I hope you'll agree the results are good, as are the words and the maps, and the information and the opinions. Please let us know if you can think of improvements, aspects we missed you'd like to know about, places we perhaps overlooked - but sorry, no, we're not doing Barrow next time. Perhaps the time after? We hope it will be regularly updated, though not as frequently as *The Good Guide.* In this book, we've tried to be more dateless, produce a longer lasting read, to be kept and treasured, which is why the format is bigger, the binding a bit better. We all hope you will enjoy it. Thanks.

Hunter Davies,
Loweswater, Easter, 1988.

Post box, Wasdale Head

A Note on Entries

Whilst compiling this book, I often thought a better title would be *At the Time of Writing* , there have been so many changes since I started it. The Lake District towns and villages are always developing, but never, it seems, so fast as in recent years. Sitting down to write a guide book is always provocation for things to plunge into a state of turmoil: No sooner had I written about them than the Bowness Bay cushion huts were demolished; I abused the Walter Wilson supermarket in Ulverston, only to discover that they are now planning to build another one somewhere else; similarly, * the Co-Op in Brogden Street had decided it was time to move after goodness knows how many years; Kendal high street is pockmarked with building society offices and empty shop fronts and the whole of the Lake District is suddenly awash with estate agents, sheltered housing and timeshare developments (not to mention that blight of rural areas, the empty holiday cottage, about which I have been manfully restrained throughout).

It is sad to see the heart go out of the surrounding towns, as those within the National Park grow richer through tourism. Although this book is centred on the Park, I hope it encourages the reader to explore some of the gems that lie outside the boundary.

The entries in the book are grouped in chapters tenuously linked by geographical location. It assumes that you could base yourself in the main town of each chapter and explore the rest in a weekend. This book isn't a comprehensive gazeteer (I always like to leave myself open to offers of a sequel) nor is it an in-depth study of vernacular architecture. I've tried to strike a balance by exploring the places I find interesting, or which a visitor to the area is likely to encounter. There are probably places which I shall kick myself for leaving out, in a month or so. The opinions (apart from those in the appendix) are all mine. Don't take them too seriously and feel free to disagree violently (letters to Forster Davies Limited).

Details of places to visit - such as opening times and prices - change so rapidly, there's no point in trying to include them here. For more information, refer to *The Good Guide to the Lakes* or the nearest tourist information centre. Similarly, events information can only be general. In all entries, I've indicated the nearest source of tourist information (but note that the smaller centres, such as those in shops at Sawrey, Lorton and Elterwater) aren't really equipped to handle long, complicated enquiries over the telephone.

Walks are given for the major entries, in most cases starting from

---

* for asterisk read "at the time of writing"

the town or village centre. The routes are indications only; consult an Ordnance Survey map for more detail. * all the restaurants and hotels mentioned were in business and thriving, but they do come and go. Again, *The Good Guide* has more up to date details.

Ratings   In common with *The Good Guide* , we've rated each entry according to the following system: stars for attractiveness, interest, atmosphere, etc. and letters as a rough guide to the amount of time you can spend there (*without* allowing time to do the walks, visit the museums, park the car, etc.). Full ratings are as follows:-

A	4 hours or more	***	Not to be missed
B	2 to 3 hours	**	Highly recommended
C	1 hour or less	*	Interesting

Maps   These are sketch maps, indicating the layout of streets, places of interest, most attractive parts of town. They're not to scale and are the result of meandering around with a sketchbook and a compass (and feeling rather foolish in the process). In most instances, North is at the top of the map (just in case you have an overriding urge to get a compass and do the same ...). * all the streets and buildings were in place, but it's several days since I was in some of the towns, so you can never tell.

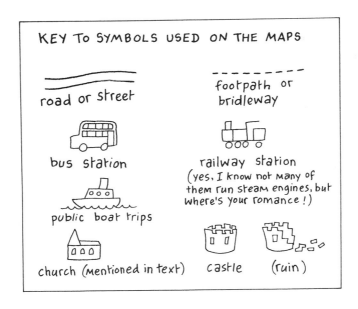

9

Bowness Bay

Chapter 1

WINDERMERE

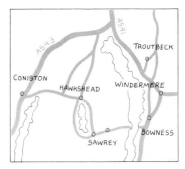

Bowness and Windermere

FLAVOUR

Bowness and Windermere began life as two separate villages. Today you can hardly tell where one finishes and the other begins. It causes visitors no end of confusion, especially if they turn up at Windermere railway station expecting to see the lake, only to discover that it is a mile and a half down the road.

Bowness is more properly called Bowness-on-Windermere, to distinguish it from the other Bowness, up on the Solway coast. For many people it is their first view of the Lake District. This is both a Good Thing and a Bad Thing. On the one hand, there is the lake close at hand, with panoramic views across the bay to Helvellyn and the Langdales. On a quiet evening in Spring or early Autumn it can be very attractive.

On the other hand, because it is so easy to get to, and because the views can be so nice, many people go no further and the whole village has become very touristy. At the height of summer it can seem more like Blackpool than the Lake District. Bowness Bay becomes the sea front, awash with hordes of people clutching ice creams. The pavements become so crowded that pedestrians spill off into the roads, turning driving into a game of dodgems. Coaches full of day-trippers clutter up the front, sometimes parking two deep and performing elaborate manouvers that hold up the traffic. It is no great surprise that one of the common questions asked in the information centre is: "Where is the National Park?"

First impressions of Bowness are not encouraging. The village seems full of shops selling slate ornamental name plates (for people who live in houses called Rydal or Wetherlam), genuine local Scottish woollen shops and, for some reason, dress shops. Ash Street becomes so horrible it's known as the Kazbah. However, it really is very easy to escape it all. Just follow Glebe Road down to Cockshott Point, or climb up Brantfell Road and take the footpath to Post Knott and within minutes the crowds seem a million miles away.

11

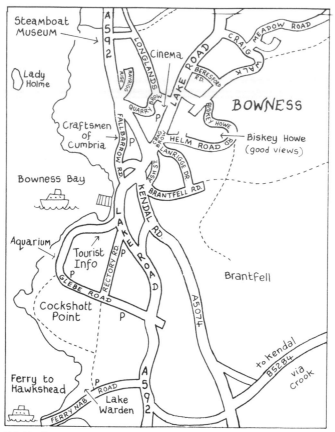

FACTS

The oldest part of Bowness is the area between St Martin's Church and the lake shore, known as Lowside. Hemmed in by The Old England Hotel to the south and Fallbarrow Caravan Park at the north, this jumble of houses and tiny streets is all that remains of the original village. This area was once little more than a cluster of fishermens' huts, sheltered against the hillside. The best way to explore it is on foot. Park in Rayrigg Road and wander south along Fallbarrow Road, bearing left at the snooker club. (This was once a model railway exhibition. It closed a few years ago but is still haunted the the sad spectacle of middle-aged men in raincoats forlornly searching for the model trains ...)

It won't take long before you come across the New Hall Inn, known locally as the Hole int' Wall (because it was once possible to hand ale through a window direct to the smithy next door). The Hole is one of the original three inns which stood on the old road through Bowness. The others were The Stag's Head, just behind the church, (look for the sign,

12

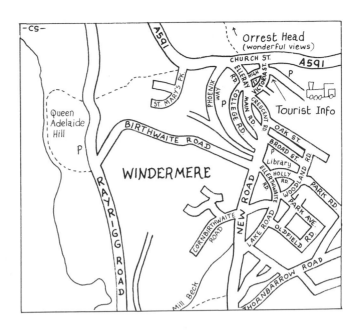

'Post Horses for Hire' - contrasting strangely with the warning that leather jackets and helmets may not be worn into the disco) and the Royal Oak Inn on Brantfell Road (originally called The Ship Inn, hence the ship on the sign). Charles Dickens once stayed at the Hole int' Wall.

The promenade is worth exploring for the old boating huts, also called cushion huts. There have been huts on this site since the turn of the century when the tourist industry was just getting started and rowing boats were first hired along here. (The huts were last rebuilt at the beginning of 1988.) There's another reminder of this period across in the Information Centre, in the form of a fabulous beast known as a Tizzie Wizzie. The old boatmen used to get visitors hunting for these under the piers at dusk, as a way of promoting their boats. A bizarre cross between a bird and a hedgehog, with a squirrel's tail thrown in for good measure, the specimen in the centre still fools people. You can understand the Japanese accepting it at face value but you'd think with a legacy of David Attenborough wildlife programmes on tv the British would spot the joke ...

The promenade is overlooked by the Belsfield Hotel, an imposing white building with attractive lawns which sweep down to a high wall by the main road. This was once the home of the Furness industrialist, H. W. Schneider. To reach his offices at Barrow, he used to commute from Bowness via steam launch and train. His launch, *The Esperance*, gave its name to the smaller of the two piers.

The Belsfield is one of a number of grand buildings which sprang

The old 'cushion huts' at Bowness Bay

up with arrival of the New Wealthy; industrialists from Lancashire who built splendid mansions along the east shore of Lake Windermere. The National Park Visitor Centre, Brockhole, a few miles north of Bowness, was another. It belonged to a Manchester industrialist named Gaddum.

The explosive growth of Bowness as a tourist resort was the direct result of the railway opening up at Windermere. But if Bowness grew, Windermere was created. Well, in name at any rate. Before the railway arrived in 1848, there was only a tiny hamlet called Birthwaite. The railway station put Windermere on the map. Even if it was a mile and a half from where it should have been.

Windermere has much more of a residential air about it than Bowness. You don't get the feeling that the entire village is going to pack up its bags and head south once the season is over. The shops contain one or two oddities; there's a doll's shop in College Road, which sells and repairs old Victorian dolls. The large building in the centre of the main street (between the two one-way bits) was once the Embassy Cinema. Peer up at the wall on the northern end, above the shop doorway, and there is an inscription which reads Acme House. Not, as far as is known, anything to do with Roadrunner cartoons.

BEST BUILDINGS

In Bowness, definitely **St Martin's Church**. It is the parish church of Windermere and was built around 1483, replacing a much earlier church which was destroyed by fire. It looks oddly out of place in the middle of all the traffic and hubbub, but manages to preserve a certain dignity, screened from St. Martin's Square by trees. The inside is well worth investigating. The font and some of the stained glass survived from the original church and may once have come from Cartmel Priory.

Another fascinating building is on an island in the middle of the lake. This is the famous round house on **Belle Isle**. Said to be the only completely circular house in the country. It was built in 1774 by Thomas English. Seven years later, the island was bought by Isabella Curwen and named after her (it was originally called Longholme). It is still lived in by the Curwen family and used to be open to the public, with boat trips from Bowness Bay. There is no longer public access to the island but you can get a good view of the house from Cockshot Point or the ferry.

Half-way between Bowness and Windermere, on Lake Road, is a squat clock tower. This is known as **Baddeley's Clock**, a memorial to M. J. B. Baddeley, the famous guide-book writer. He died in 1906 and his grave, in Bowness cemetery, has a headstone made from rock brought from the summit of Scafell Pike.

Some of the inns are worth looking at, especially the **Royal Oak** on Brantfell Road (not the Royal Hotel). For fans of the architect Voysey, there is **Broadleys**, a few miles south of Bowness on the A590. Now the headquarters of the Windermere Motor Boat Club and not open to the public. It featured in the film *The French Lieutenant's Woman*.

THINGS TO DO

Windermere Steamboat Museum, Rayrigg Road (Windermere 5565). Excellent collection of old steam craft, including , the Osprey and the Kittiwake, which take passengers for trips on the lake.

Lake Windermere Aquarium, Glebe Road (Windermere 4585). Small and slightly eccentric enterprise, with an amazing array of freshwater fish, typical of the ones found in Lake Windermere (including the dreaded pike). Also features a small shop.

Craftsmen of Cumbria, Fallbarrow Road (Windermere 2959). More of a shop really, but some nice displays and exhibitions, including a model railway. You can see craftspeople at work and try your hand at brass rubbing and poker work. Free to get in and there is a pleasant cafe on site.

Lakeland Experience, Lowside (Windermere 2223). Bowness's own multi-slide audio-visual show. Not quite on a par with the London Experience and you don't have to wander far to see the Real Thing, but a possibility for a wet half-hour.

Brockhole, The National Park Visitor Centre (Windermere 6601). Open every day throughout the season and always a lot going on. For details of daily events, pick up a list at any tourist information centre.

Evenings: Royalty Cinema, Lake Road (Windermere 3364). Good for the latest blockbusters, with matinees during the school holidays, especially if wet.

Theatre: no established theatre as such, but there is a local company, The Windermere Players, who put on productions, especially during The Windermere Festival. Otherwise, the nearest theatres are Theatre-in-the-Forest, Grizedale, or The Brewery Arts Centre, Kendal.

Lectures/talks: regular programme held in **The Countryside Threatre,** in Bowness Bay tourist information centre, during the summer. Full details in the National Park's *Lake District Guardian,* a free newspaper available from all tourist information centres in the area.

EVENTS

Lake Windermere Festival - usually held in early July and last around eight days. Not exactly culture, but a lot going on at both Bowness and Ambleside.

Windermere Marathon - a circuit of the Lake, starting and finishing in Bowness, usually with large numbers of contestants from all over the country. Held on a Sunday in late October. Further details nearer the time from the local information centres.

WALKS

You need transport to get to the high fells, but there are some nice low level walks. From Bowness, a good way to escape the crowds is to take the ferry to the other side of the lake (very cheap for pedestrians) and walk up Claife, or just along the lake shore. Good wooded walk which can take you almost to Ambleside, joining the main road at Wray Castle (not a real castle - see Ambleside entry). Again from Bowness, head up Brantfell Road and across the fields at the top to reach an attractive wooded footpath which takes you to Post Knott, a good viewpoint. In fact, from here you can link up with the Dales Way and head out to Yorkshire, if you're feeling energetic. Biskey Howe is another excellent viewpoint, with views to the head of the lake.

Windermere's best walk is undoubtably up to Orrest Head. The path starts opposite the tourist information centre and after twenty minutes or so you find yourself at one of the best viewpoints in the area. Splendid views all round, to the high fells, across to the Pennines or back to the coast at Morcambe Bay. Again, a footpath link can take you right through to Ambleside, via Troutbeck; a good seven mile hike - time it to come back to Bowness via one of the steamers or launches.

STAYING

Wide choice of accomodation, to many to list here - from cheapie B&B to the luxurious surroundings of the **Miller Howe** (Windermere 2536). *Hint:* if going up market, try some of the small country house hotels outside the village, such as **The Lindeth Fell** (Windermere 3286). If coming up for the weekend in mid-summer, it is vital to book in advance as it can get very busy, especially at bank holidays and extra-especially if you want to be close to the lake. Bowness and Windermere aren't particularly handy for the northern lakes; allow about an hour's drive

Stained glass window in St Martin's Church, Bowness

17

to Keswick. More if you're trying to get through Ambleside in the middle of summer.

Best time to come - probably late Autumn. Things quieten down a bit towards the end of October, the trees are turning and most of the visitor attractions are still open. Spring is okay but the weather can be dodgy and some places haven't opened up yet. The place is starting to get very busy in weekends in February and March, but mostly with day-trippers so accomodation isn't a problem.

EATING

Bowness and Windermere must have between them the best collection of decent restaurants in the National Park. There's the famous **Miller Howe** (Windermere 2536) on Rayrigg Road, **Roger's Restaurant** (Windermere 4954) on High Street, the **Porthole** (Windermere 2793) in Ash Street; three of the best restaurants in the area. Also, some of the smaller hotels are good for evening meals. The area is less good for decent cafes. For light lunches try **Hedgerow** (Windermere 5002) or the new Miller Howe-run cafe at **Lakeland Plastics** (Windermere 2255).

TRANSPORT

Well placed for transport. Windermere is the only village in Central Lakeland with rail connections to the outside world, and a dinky new railway station to match (it looks as if it came straight out of Beatrix Potter). Train times onWindermere 3025 or to Oxenholme on Kendal 20397. Good bus links to Ambleside, Coniston, Hawkshead, Keswick, Kendal and Lancaster, run by Ribble (Kendal 20932). **The Mountain Goat** is a coach tour company which also operates a straightforward passenger service to Ullswater (Windermere 5161). And don't forget the Lake steamers and launches, which are a good means of getting to Lakeside, in the south, or Ambleside, in the north: **Windermere Iron Steamboat Company** - they run the big steamers (Newby Bridge 31539); **Bowness Bay Boating Company** - who run the smaller launches (Windermere 3360).

By car, only 45 minutes or so from the M6 (junction 36). Parking can be a problem in Bowness. Restricted parking on the main streets and you can never find a space anyway. The best car park is in Rayrigg Road, which puts you in the centre of things. Or try Braithwaite Fold, on the other side of Glebe Road; it opens for parking during the summer months only. Windermere tends to be a bit quieter, but not much. Restricted street parking, but slightly less hopeless than Bowness (try College Road). Unless you are shopping there, don't be tempted to usethe car park at Booths supermarket; they're red hot with the wheel clamps. There is also a good car park in Broad Street, behind the library.

If you want to get across the lake, just south of Bowness is a car ferry which crosses every fifteen minutes, throughout the day, seven days a week. Around 90p. per car (at the time of writing), even cheaper for pedestrians and cyclists. It can get very busy in summer though, with long queues (there are signs by the road telling you how long you have to wait). Go early, come back late. Watch finishing times if you're on foot or cycle - usually around 10pm - check times with the tourist information centre at Bowness Bay. Can be a long walk if you miss it.

Tourist Information Centres Bowness Bay National Park Information Centre, Glebe Road (Windermere2895). Windermere tourist information centre, Victoria Street (6499). Both operate an accomodation booking service.

By the way, if you really want to know whether you're in Windermere or Bowness, the official boundary follows the line of Mill Beck.

Edwardian gentlemen, excitedly hunting the Tizzy-Wizzy

Bowness Bay.   Boat Landings.

Troutbeck

FLAVOUR

Troutbeck is really a cluster of hamlets, stretched out along the road, and originally forming around a series of small wells. There is no real focus to the village, though the area around the post office and Robin Lane is as good as you'll get. It is a picturesque setting, with the fells to the east forming a very dramatic backdrop. The village itself is fairly business-like and doesn't give the impression of going in for much frivolity.

FACTS

Troutbeck valley runs northwards from Windermere towards Ullswater, the road climbing out over the Kirkstone Pass. To the west is Wansfell, to the east Kentmere. At the head of the valley stands High Street. The village itself is on the west side of the valley, strung out along a narrow, undulating minor road, which runs parallel to the main A592. It is rich farming country, with a lot of sheep farming. Good place to wander about in the hope of seeing working sheepdogs.

The Roman road from Penrith to Ambleside crossed High Street and must have descended through Troutbeck valley, though its exact course has been lost. Still a number of pack horse routes obvious (such as Garburn Pass, over to Kentmere Valley). The village grew up based on agriculture. There was some slate quarrying in the eighteenth century. The original farmhouses date back to the seventeenth century, but the arrival of the Windermere railway brought in the Manchester merchants and a number of larger houses were built. The two inns were rebuilt around this time.

BEST BUILDINGS

Great for vernacular architecture buffs (that's local native buildings). The whole village has an air of being frozen in time; a working example of the nineteenth century. Don't let this put you off. One of the oldest houses in Troutbeck is **Townend**. Originally a statesman farmer's house, dating from 1626. It remained in the Browne family until it was given to the National Trust in 1947. In addition to the exterior charm (note the old round chimneys), the inside has been restored to its former glory, with original furniture and fine oak panelling.

Look out for bank barns, a peculiarity of hilly, upland areas like the Lake District. These two-storey barns are built along the contours of a hill, usually allowing access from the farmyard into the lower section,

Townend

for housing livestock, and access to the top floor from the slope behind. The upper floor is often a grain store or threshing barn. Carts can be driven in straight off the slope. It was at one time the main type of farm building in the Lakes. Examples can be seen all over the area. There is one beside the post office, at the turning to Robin Lane.

The **Mortal Man Hotel** is interesting. Originally called The White House Inn, built in 1689. It was renamed sometime around the beginning of the eighteenth century and now bears a sign with the peculiar rhyme:

> *O mortal man, that lives by bread,*
> *What is it that makes thy nose so red?*
> *Thou silly fool, that looks't so pale,*
> *'Tis drinking Sally Birkett's ale.*

The original sign was painted by Julius Caesar Ibbotson, who lived for a time at Clappersgate, near Ambleside. The current sign is an imitation, the original having been lost.

Whilst you are wandering about, also look out for the wells. They are situated in the wall beside the road, on the west side. A number of them are dedicated to various saints.

21

THINGS TO DO

Town End (Ambleside 32628). Owned by the NT and open during the summer season. One of the most interesting Lakeland houses open to the public. No electric lighting to spoil the ambiance.

WALKS

From the head of the valley, you can walk up along Trout Beck and over Threshwaite Cove to Hartsop, or up onto High Street. Another good route is to follow the 'Garburn Road' across to Kentmere. For the less ambitious, a footpath just south of the church takes you over Far Orrest and Orrest Head to Windermere, or you can follow Robin Lane (just by the post office) and walk to Ambleside. Nanny Lane (behind Lane Foot Farm) takes you up onto Wansfell and some superb views.

STAYING

One ot two small B&Bs, otherwise try the **Queen's Head Hotel** (Ambleside 32174), or the **Mortal Man Hotel** (Ambleside 33193) - the latter probably the quieter of the two. Handy for Bowness and Windermere, but nicely tucked out of the way in real countryside.

EATING

Either of the two inns, above. Mortal Man is possibly the better of the two.

TRANSPORT

Only two-and-a-half miles from Windermere, so you could walk. The only public transport is by the Mountain Goat. They run a regular daily service from Ambleside to Glenridding (via Windermere and Troutbeck) in the summer. Very limited car parking, though the two pubs have a fair amount of space.

Tourist information   Windermere tourist information centre.

Sawrey

Sawrey consists of two bits - Near Sawrey and Far Sawrey. If you're travelling from Bowness, Far Sawrey is the nearest and Near Sawrey the farthest. They were named from the Hawkshead direction. They're really two small hamlets, consisting of a few large Victorian houses and the occasional farm, strung out along the back road between Hawkshead and the ferry. Neat, attractive hamlets in nice countryside for rambling.

Near Sawrey is most famous for **Hill Top**, Beatrix Potter's house. In fact, she owned loads of houses and farms in this area, most of which went to the National Trust upon her death in 1943. She bought Hill Top farm in 1905 with the proceeds from the sale of the first of her 'little tales', *Peter Rabbit* . The countryside around Sawrey is easily recognised from the illustrations in her books. The house itself featured in *Jemima Puddleduck* . It is tucked away behind a farm in the centre of the village.

Near Sawrey is also renowned for the Tower Bank Arms; a pleasant old pub owned by the National Trust. Good for bar meals.

THINGS TO DO

Hill Top (Hawkshead 334). Owned and run by the National Trust and open to the public (one of the most visited properties in Lakeland, averaging around 90,000 visitors a year). Her original paintings are now on display in Hawkshead, at the **Beatrix Potter Gallery**.

Grizedale Visitor Centre, Grizedale Forest (Satterthwaite 272). Small Forestry Commission visitor centre devoted to the history and ecology of Grizedale. Recently greatly improved with new displays and an attractive craft shop.

Evenings: Theatre-in-the-Forest, Grizedale (Satterthwaite 291). Small theatre on the road between Satterthwaite and Hawkshead. Stages small-scale concerts and theatrical performances all year round.

WALKS

There is a good walk from Bowness to Sawrey, crossing via the car ferry. Plan your route to use the footpaths rather than the roads, though the latter remain pretty quiet most of the year. Alternatively, there are guided walks from Bowness Bay Information Centre, some of which aim for Hill Top - and you get the benefit of local knowledge. Details in the *Lake District Guardian*. If walking around Claife Heights, take a map and compass - it is a maze of conflicting trails and a short ramble can quickly turn into a major orienteering event.

STAYING & EATING

Try the **Sawrey Hotel** (Windermere 3425), at Far Sawrey. One or two farms around doing B&B. You're nicely out of the way at Sawrey, but bear in mind the time of the last ferry if you go across to Bowness for the evening.

For good pub food, try the **Tower Bank Arms** (Hawkshead 334). **The Drunken Duck** (Hawkshead 347) is also worth investigating, three miles north, on the Hawkshead to Ambleside road.

TRANSPORT

Ho, ho. One bus a week, on a Wednesday. Travels between Hawkshead and the ferry landing, at Ferry House. Nice cycling country. The popularity of Hill Top can make car parking a bit of a problem in the village. A few spaces by the Tower Banks Arms.

Tourist information available at the sub-post office, Far Sawrey.

Hawkshead

FLAVOUR

One of South Lakeland's most popular small towns. It's not too difficult to see why. It has an 'olde worlde' charm which is quite unlike anything else in the area. Two neat, interlinked squares, a maze of quaint streets, timber-framed buildings that overhang the pavement. Add to that the connection with Wordsworth's schooldays and the pulling power is complete.

Hawkshead is like an advertisement for the National Trust, who own a good proportion of the shops and houses. It has a preserved air. It would not look out of place in a museum, like the street scene in the Castle Museum at York. This effect is heightened by the fact that cars are banned from the village centre and rerouted via the bypass.

FACTS

Hawkshead is an ancient township which stood in Lancashire, until local Government reorganisation. It was an important wool town in Norman times and during the middle ages was a grange, belonging to Furness Abbey. The monastry smelted iron in the Dalton area and the woods around Hawkshead were a rich source of charcoal. The monks owned Hawkshead Hall, just outside the town. After the dissolution of the monastries, Hawkshead grew as a market town - the first charter was granted by James I. You can judge its success by the fact that the village once had seven inns. Most of the present buildings in Hawkshead date from the seventeenth century.

After the death of his father, and a short period boarding with guardians in Penrith, William Wordsworth was sent to the grammar school at Hawkshead, which had an enviable reputation at the time. He lodged with Anne Tyson - possibly for a short time in the town itself, but for most of his stay at her home in Colthouse, the tiny hamlet just outside Hawkshead.

Cottages at Hawkshead

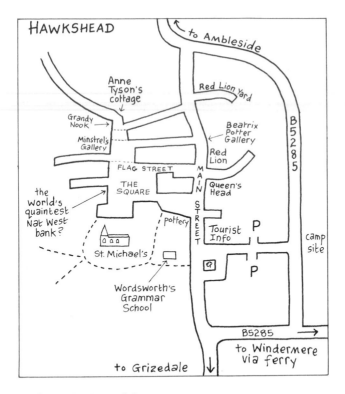

BEST BUILDINGS

Towering above the amusing jumble of houses is the parish church, **St Michael's** (nothing to do with retail chains). It stands on an unexpected hill, right in the village centre. It is saved from having an aloof, snooty air by the pleasant green churchyard and the wonderful view over the village and surrounding countryside. Some of the parish records are fascinating; there are more than two hundred 'burial in wool' certificates (one of which hangs by the north door) - these were the result of an act of Parliament which insisted on woollen shrouds for the dead - as a stimulus to the wool industry. The church is sixteenth century, with some seventeenth century improvements. There was once a Norman church in Hawkshead, but nothing now remains of it. The pseudo Anglo-Saxon cross in the churchyard is really a 1919 war memorial, designed by the famous local historian, W. G. Collingwood.

The **Grammar School** is very attractive; originally endowed by Edwin Sandys around 1575. (Sandys was a local man who went on to become Archbishop of York. There is an alter-tomb to him in the church.) The present building dates from around 1675, with eighteenth and nineteenth century additions. Anne Tyson's cottage (where Wordsworth may have stayed) is privately owned. Now called

The Queen's Head, Hawkshead

Wordsworth Lodge (ugh), it stands opposite the Grandy Nook tea-rooms.

One of the oldest buildings in Hawkshead is the **Red Lion Inn**; it was a fifteenth century coaching house. Look out for the two small figures on the wall, below the eaves - one shows a farmer taking a pig to market, the other a man with a whistle.

THINGS TO DO

Plenty of gifte-type shops, and enough sheepskin on sale to kit out an entire pack of wolves. Good bookshop. The **Esthwaite Pottery** showroom is open to the public, just past Sun Cottage.

Hawkshead Grammar School (no telephone). Wordsworth's old school. See the desk where he carved his initials. Quiet little place, with exhibits upstairs. Try and get it to yourself and chat to the guide.

Beatrix Potter Gallery (no telephone number at the time of writing). A newly-opened gallery in the former solicitor's office of her husband, William Heelis. There is an exhibition telling the story of Beatrix Potter's life and work and - at last - displays of some of her original drawings and watercolours. These are exquisite and shouldn't be missed.

Evenings: Evening music recitals in the church during the summer. Two miles down the road is the **Theatre-in-the-Forest** (see Sawrey).

EVENTS

Hawkshead Show - a small agricultural show, held late August.

WALKS

There is a pleasant walk out onto Hawkshead Moor, to the south-west. Or there are paths onto Claife, to the east (but see warnings under Sawrey, above). Very good 360 degree viewpoint at Latterbarrow. One of the nicest areas to head for is Tarn Howes; one of Lakeland's most famous beauty spots. Gets very busy at weekends and one of the few countryside areas where you have to pay to park your car. But good views and lovely if you can get it to yourself by going in the evening.

STAYING

Good range of B&B and guest houses. Hawkshead is at its best when it has quietened down in the evening, when you can stroll around and enjoy the streets and visit a pub or two. This makes it a good place to base yourself, but warned that it gets packed with visitors during the day. Handy camping and caravan site, right on the edge of the village. Doesn't do wonders for the view, but if you are backpacking and want to stay somewhere with easy access to shops and the pubs, Hawkshead is one of the better bets (also see Coniston).

EATING

Good for teas and light lunches - try the **Minstral Gallery** (Hawkshead 423) or the **Grandy Nook** (Hawkshead 404). Evenings catered for by pub meals; the **Queen's Head** (Hawkshead 271) does some of the best bar food in the Lake District.

TRANSPORT

Bus service to Ambleside and Coniston, about every two hours at last count. Otherwise you are on your own. Parking okay if you can get into the large car park on the east of the village, just off the B5286. Good access to Bowness if you use the ferry, otherwise half-an-hour's drive around the top of the lake.

Tourist information National Park information centre by the car park (Hawkshead 525).

Coniston

FLAVOUR

Coniston village stands slightly off the main tourist track through the Lake District, but still manages to attract more than its fair share of the visitors. A grey, Lakeland stone village, it is overshadowed by the spectacular bulk of the Old Man, the 2631ft mountain to the west. Spectacular setting, with Coniston Water to the east.

Although the village is highly popular with visitors, it lacks any charm of its own. Whereas Bowness, Windermere and Ambleside have grown up with tourism, you get the impression that Coniston leapt onto the bandwagon rather late, just to cash in.

FACTS

The village has a strong industrial background. The area is rich in copper and iron ore; large numbers of coppiced woods testify to its importance in producing charcoal; and as the mining industry has declined, its place has been taken by slate quarrying. Mining in the Coniston area probably dates back to Roman times, but the village

Yewdale Road, Coniston

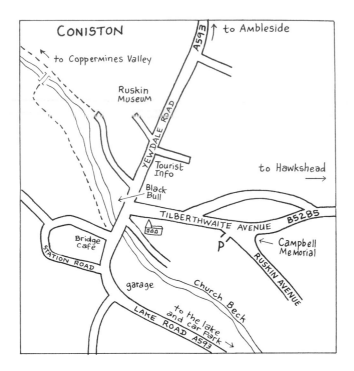

began to flourish from about the sixteenth century onwards. Miners from the Mines Royal at Keswick were brought across to work the copper mines. The village grew in importance during the eighteenth and nineteenth centuries with the development of mining at the head of Church Beck. Though now something of an industrial wasteland, the area around Church Beck is still known locally as Coppermines Valley.

Coniston used to have good transportation links with the outside world; in the early days, iron ore was transported by boat on Coniston, then by cart to Broughton-in-Furness. Coniston Water still retains its status as a public highway. Rail links arrived in the mid-eighteenth century, with the opening of a branch of the Furness line (now long gone, unfortunately).

BEST BUILDINGS

The oldest building in the village is **Coniston Hall**, which stands a mile south of the village centre, on the lake shore. It was originally a pele tower, built around 1250 by Sir Richard le Fleming. It remained the main residence of the Flemings until 1408. Sir Thomas Fleming married Isabel, heiress of Sir John de Lancaster, of Rydal, and so came into Rydal Hall. The Flemings flitted between the two for the next three centuries,

30

until they finally made up their minds to settle at Rydal. By this time, the pele tower had been converted into a large hall. In 1815, it was turned into a farmhouse. Finally, in 1972, it was bought by the National Trust. The grounds are now used as a camp site and the Hall - sometimes called Coniston Old Hall - is gradually being restored.

St Andrew's Church, in the village centre, is pleasant, if unremarkable. The original charch dated from 1586, but the present building was built in 1819. John Ruskin is buried in the churchyard and there is a memorial in the form of aa Anglo-Saxon cross, designed by W. G. Collingwood.

Ruskin settled in Coniston in 1871, at the age of 52, an area he had visited as a boy. He bought his house, **Brantwood**, sight unseen and transfered a "mere shed of rotten timbers and loose stone" into one of the most beautiful houses in the district. Brantwood stands on the eastern shore of Coniston Water, with spectacular views across the lake to the Old Man.

Yewdale Farm, two miles north of the village, is interesting for a good example of a typical Cumbrian spinning gallery. The farm is owned by the National Trust, but rented privately, so there is no public access. The gallery is, however, visible from the road.

Finally, Coppermines Valley contains some interesting relics. Depending on your point of view, the area is a splendid opportunity for industrial archeology, or a hideous eyesore which needs tidying up. However, if you're keen you can find plenty of evidence of the mining operations, including the pump house, the old wheel house and some of the leats which brought down water from Levers Water to power the machinery. A note of warning: there are still a number of mine shafts in the valley but these are definitely *not* safe to explore and should be avoided.

THINGS TO DO

One or two interesting antique shops, otherwise Coniston is mostly gift shops. Good Sunday antique market during the summer. Ring the information centre for times and dates.

Ruskin Museum, Yewdale Road (Coniston 41541). Tiny museum devoted mainly to Ruskin, including correspondence, possessions and his geology collection. Sitting rather oddly amongst all this, is a set of photographs of Donald Campbell's ill-fated world water speed record attempt, in 1967. There is a memorial to Campbell in the village, opposite the main car park.

Brantwood (Coniston 41396). One of the most spectacularly-sited houses in England. Over the past few years, Brantwood has been built up into an attraction which rivals some of the Wordsworth homes, yet remains friendly and unpressurised. The house is laid out as it was in Ruskin's time, with examples of his own sketches and paintings, as well as his personal art collection. Exhibitions of local interest and even a good cafe.

Gondola (Coniston 41288). An original steam launch which used to ply Coniston Water in the nineteenth century. Restored and run by the National Trust. Sumptuous fittings and a near silent engine make this a glorious way to see the lake and surrounding fells. *Warning:* unable to sail in rough weather, contact Coniston tourist information centre to check times.

WALKS

Assuming you're not here to tackle the big one, the Old Man itself, there are a number of good shorter walks in the vicinity. Church Beck is worth exploring - head up behind the Black Bull Inn, following a cart track to the top of the beck. From here you can explore Coppermines Valley. Return via the narrow bridge and the wooded lane on the southern bank of the river. Good access to Coniston Water on the western shore, along part of the Cumbrian Way, although you have to trek along the main road for a mile or so to get to it. Takes you past Coniston Hall, but you miss the best views. The east view caters less well for the walker, though there are a number of tiny car parks if you travel down by car. Brantwood has a good nature trail. Finally, one of the best ways onto the Old Man is along the old packhorse route, the Walna Scar road, and up onto Dow Crag. This is a Major Expedition, however, so make sure you are properly equipped and allow most of the day to do it.

STAYING

The Black Bull (Coniston 41335) is a sixteenth century coaching inn and rather attractive. Veggies should try the **Beech Tree Guest House** (Coniston 41717) in Yewdale Road. Just south of the village, at Torver is the **Wheelgate Hotel** (Coniston 41418), very prettily situated. There is a good camping site on the lake shore at Coniston Hall - one of the few within easy walking distance of a Lakeland town or village if you want to get to the pub in the evening. Coniston is a good base for exploring the southern lakes and some of the less crowded areas out to the west. Less good for the northern lakes because of the bottleneck at Ambleside.

Not Yewdale Farm, but another good spinning gallery on a cottage at nearby Tilberthwaite

EATING

Not so hot for restaurants, though a number of cafes. Try the **Bridge Cafe**, or the one at **Brantwood**. Evening meals catered for by pub meals - try the **Black Bull Inn**.

TRANSPORT

Bus links to Ambleside, Hawkshead and Ulverston, although a bit infrequent. Nice winding roads to explore by car. Allow fifteen minutes to get to Ambleside in the summer. Parking in the village can be rather fraught unless you make use of the large main car park.

Tourist information   National Park information centre in Yewdale Road (Coniston 41533).

Ambleside Rushbearing ceremony

Chapter 2

AMBLESIDE

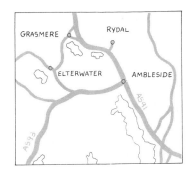

Ambleside and Waterhead B **

FLAVOUR

Let's get the misleading bit out of the way first: Waterhead is at the head of Lake Windermere. It's not Ambleside. Ambleside is a mile farther north. (Tough if nobody warned you when you got on the boat and you don't fancy the walk.) They were once two separate villages and today even have their own separate information centres (run by two separate organisations). Having said all that, you're unlikely to visit one without the other, so I've lumped them together.

Waterhead is only a tiny place. Little more than a group of hotels and the boat landings. The remains of the Roman fort are just past Borrans Park, on the bypass that takes you round to Hawkshead and Coniston. Not much to see on the ground. You get a better impression looking down from Todd Crag, on Loughrigg.

Waterhead is pleasant to stroll around on a clear summer evening, with some spectacular sunsets over the Langdales. During the day, most people press straight on to Ambleside. If you've come by boat, don't walk along the main road (unless you particularly wish to be confronted by Hayes Garden Centre), go down past the information centre and follow the road over Rothay Bridge. Turn right and the narrow lane takes you along the Under Loughrigg road. After half a mile or so you come to another bridge on your right, for pedestrians only. Cross over and this takes you into Rothay Park. Not the quickest route into Ambleside, but one of the most pleasent.

Now Ambleside. If you're travelling from the south, this is where the Lake District really begins. Dark grey Lakeland stone houses, a backdrop of mountains, a real market, a centre not entirely overrun with tourist shops ...look carefully and you'll see a real village here, struggling to get out. Oddly enough, it's an impression which doesn't break down with living here. There's a thriving community feel to Ambleside which more than compensates for the appalling traffic in summer.

Ambleside sits on the river Rothay, surrounded on three sides by Lakeland fells; to the north there's Fairfield (a Genuine Mountain, being well over 2000 feet high), to the east there's Wansfell (nearly a mountain at over 1500 feet and Not To Be Underestimated), and in the west is Loughrigg (only a fell really, but good for afternoon rambles and evening strolls). Start climbing any one of these and you get a good picture of Ambleside as a tiny cluster of houses, dwarfed by mountains.

The impression breaks down if you're stuck in the car, crawling along Compston Road at 0.002 mph and trying to get to Keswick in time to do Borrowdale. Ambleside can be quite horrendous for traffic, a real bottleneck if you're heading north. There have been rumours of a bypass for years, but that would wreck the surrounding countryside. There's only one solution - be out early and get through before ten o'clock (for further ravings, see Transport, below.)

There are one or two nice corner shop-style shops (i.e. what everyone thinks of as a typical English corner shop, but without the corner). By contrast, Zefferelli's Arcade is a swisher, modern development, situated under the Cinema in what used to be grotty old auction rooms. The brainchild of Ambleside's resident entrepreneur and cinema manager, Derek Hook, it's decidedly upmarket and worth investigating.

The village is greatly favoured by the climbing fraternity. The proper sort, not the wellies and plastic raincoat brigade. These are real men (and women) who wear tracksuit trousers with stripes on and carry empty chalk bags about with them on the streets. In fact, there are so many climbing and outdoor shops in the village (five at the last count), that you can't really consider yourself streetwise in Ambleside unless you're dressed in the latest high technology, breathable raingear, carrying a rucksack and wearing heavy walking boots - and that's just for a trip down to the chippie.

FACTS

The oldest part of Ambleside lies on the east side of the Rothay, on Chapel Hill. Walk from the market cross towards the Salutation Hotel and turn up North Road. Continue up North Road and you come to Smithy Brow, which takes you onto Kirkstone Road. This area around here has a maze of narrow roads with tiny, interesting cottages; a group called How Head date back to the fifteenth and seventeenth centuries. Almost opposite the tiny garden centre in North Road, there's a tiny alley way (or 'snicket') on the left which takes you down by the river - look out for the restored waterwheel and the castellated house. There were once five mills, clustered along the length of Stock Ghyll.

There has been a settlement of sorts at this point since Roman times; they established a fort just south of Ambleside, called Galava. It defended the road which crossed High Street from Brougham and went across Hard Knott to Ravenglass. The medieval village grew up on the pack horse route over Kirkstone. Once the market charter was granted in 1650 (making Grasmere residents jealous), the focus of the village moved down to the area of the market cross. There is still a weekly market, held on Wednesdays; now rather tiny and tucked away in the car park behind Church Street.

When tourism hit the area, the Victorians made straight for Stock Ghyll Force and started gushing about wild, picturesque beauty, doing their usual trick of sticking up bridges so that everyone could come and appreciate how wild and unspoilt it was. There's even a turnstile at the top. When they settled down and started building, the village grew down towards the Rothay and towards Waterhead. Hayes Garden Centre is - despite its appearance - a fairly traditional part of town, the original garden centre dates back nearly a hundred years.

Ambleside has many literary connections. Harriet Martineau, the diarist and close friend of Wordsworth, lived here. Dr Thomas Arnold, headmaster of Rugby School, had a house nearby and Charlotte Mason gave her name to the teacher-training college in the centre of the village.

BEST BUILDINGS

Not the biggest, not the most picturesque, but certainly the most famous is the **Bridge House**, which stands over Stock Beck in Bridge Street. This peculiar little construction must have featured on more Lakeland postcards than just about anything else (with the possible exceptions of Ashness Bridge and Wordsworth's daffodils). Now it is a National Trust shop, but at various times it has been a weaver's shop, family home, cobblers and a tiny tea room. Legend has it that it was built by a Scotsman to avoid land tax, which is a nice idea but in reality it was the apple store for Ambleside Hall when this area was all orchard.

St Mary's Church is quite pleasant, built in the mid-nineteenth century and tucked away at the bottom end of Compston Road. The steeple soars above the surrounding rooftops when viewed from Wansfell or Loughrigg. The style caused much controversy when it was built but now it is hard to see why (especially compared to the ghastly building that now guards the entrance to the tennis courts and completely dominates the view down Compston Road).

So far, most of the new estates in Ambleside have been discretely tucked away on the hillside above the village, where you never come across them unless you are really looking. One recent eyesore is the Millans Court building, behind Zefferelli's. It used to be a garage but now a sheltered housing development has arisen, resembling Colditz.

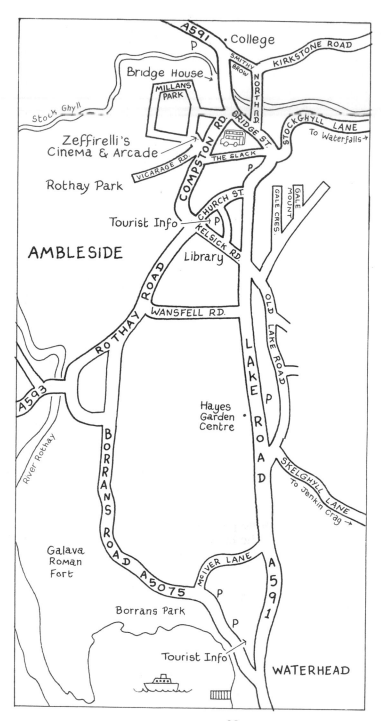

Another piece of architectural ghastliness is Quaysider's, at Waterhead. A holiday timeshare, it trumpets its presence with a sign which would not be out of place on the sea front at Blackpool. (The National Park planners do seem to have problems restricting some of the ghastly signs which are starting to spring up all over the Lakes.)

Wray Castle, just south of Ambleside on the B5286 to Hawkshead, is worth investigating for curiosity value. From a distance it looks like a medieval castle, but on closer inspection it turns out to be a Victorian folly. Beatrix Potter stayed here on holiday when she was sixteen. Owned by the National Trust but leased by the Wray Castle College of Marine Electronics. The gardens and part of the house are open to the public (telephone Ambleside 32320).

THINGS TO DO

Nothing in the way of museums or art galleries, though Ambleside did once have a Doll's House Museum and a place called the Lakeland Heritage Centre. Now both closed down, alas (well, the Heritage Centre wasn't a huge loss). But Ambleside is so handy for everywhere else in the South Lakes that it hardly matters. Especially handy for **Brockhole**, the National Park Visitor Centre, just down the road towards Windermere. You can get to it by launch from Waterhead, which makes a nice way to spend an afternoon.

One or two craft shops and the aforementioned **Zefferelli's Arcade**. There's always **Hayes Garden Centre**, between Waterhead and Ambleside. A massive place, promoting itself as Cumbria's Crystal Palace. Good for an hour or so pottering amongst the plants and wondering how on earth the place got planning permission.

Stagshaw Gardens, just south of Ambleside on the A591, is worth visiting in the Spring. Open April to June, daily. Owned and run by the National Trust and a nice display of rhododendrons, azaleas, magnolias in about eight acres of woodland. (Telephone Ambleside 33265.)

Evenings: Zefferelli's Cinema, Compston Road (Ambleside 33845). A delightful little place, run by an enthusiast. In addition to the summer blockbusters, Zeff's is more inclined to get some of the more esoteric films which normally don't seem to struggle north of Milton Keynes. Also managed one or two world premiers in recent years (Ken Russell's *Gothic* was one).

No established theatre - occasional performances at **Charlotte Mason College**. Watch their noticeboard for music events; they get some good performers and the venue has a friendly, intimate air. Zeff's also stages the odd concert - usually rock or jazz - and the Ambleside Players feature in summer.

EVENTS

Good for traditional events. **Ambleside Sports**, held in early August, is one of the biggest traditional sporting events in the Lake District (probably second only to Grasmere). Lots of traditional sports, such as Cumberland and Werstmorland wrestling, fell racing, etc. Held in Rydal Park, just north of Ambleside on the A591.

Ambleside Rushbearing is also worth seeing. Held at St Mary's Church on the first Saturday in July (for more details of the rushbearing ceremony, see the entry for Grasmere).

Finally, Ambleside is the host to the **Lake District Summer Music Festival**. It features music and arts events, with the emphasis on classical music. Large number of concerts held at Charlotte Mason, but also at Theatre-in-the-Forest, Grizedale (Satterthwaite 291) and Kendal Leisure Centre.

WALKS

Ambleside makes a splendid centre for low level walking. Behind the Salutation Hotel is a narrow wooded lane which leads up to Stock Ghyll Force. A very attractive waterfall and good for a half-hour's ramble. Or you could carry on and climb Wansfell. This is more of an expedition, however, so allow a couple of hours and take waterproofs (low technology ones will do). The view from Wansfell Pike is superb and takes in the whole of Lake Windermere. A good circular route takes you down the back of Wansfell to Troutbeck. Head south for half-a-mile and back up Robin Lane to skirt the foot of Wansfell and drop back into Ambleside. On the way, you pass Jenkin Crag, just south of Waterhead. This is another good viewpoint and fairly easy to get to from Ambleside or Waterhead, if you're feeling less energetic.

On the other side of Ambleside is Loughrigg. Go through Rothay Park to the Under Loughrigg road and just north of the footbridge you will find a cart track which leads you up onto the fell. Again, good views and you can spend a good couple of hours wandering around here, getting hopelessly lost without too much danger.

Fairfield lies to the north of the village, for real mountaineers, but there is a very good low level walk which gets you into the mountains. This starts off behind Charlotte Mason College. Turn off Smithy Brow and follow the narrow lane past the college, climbing above the village until you come to Nook End Farm. Continue along the footpath beyond this and you will eventually arrive at Sweden Bridge, a very attractive packhorse bridge. Cross over and head back down the narrow lane to

Ambleside. This makes a great walk for a Sunday afternoon, timing it to be back in the village in time to visit the odd tea shop ...

STAYING

A good range of guest houses and larger hotels; possibility of lake views at Waterhead but make sure you ask which side the bedroom is on. **Kirkstone Foot Hotel** (Ambleside 32232) and the **Rothay Manor** (Ambleside 33605), both on the outskirts of Ambleside, are highly recommended.

Very good access to the rest of the South Lakes, and if you're staying in Ambleside you've no excuse for not being out early and away to the north before the traffic builds up.

EATING

Sheila's Cafe (Ambleside 33079) in the Slack is good for pretty afternoon teas, but don't feel too intimidated if you're wearing wellies. **Zefferelli's** (Ambleside 33845) has an excellent Garden Cafe which is popular with the locals, also a good Wholefood Pizzeria upstairs (no, he's not paying me to say all this). Also try **Harvest** (Ambleside 33151), in Compston Road. Good for vegetarians. Excellent evening meals at the **Rothay Manor Hotel** and the **Kirkstone Foot Hotel**.

TRANSPORT

If you're relying on public transport to get about during your holiday, then Ambleside is an excellent base. Good bus links to Keswick, Grasmere, Windermere and Kendal (every hour), also to Hawkshead and Coniston (every two hours). Mountain Goat picks up in Ambleside, with a range of tours and regular runs through to Glenridding and Patterdale. Also boats from Waterhead to Brockhole, Bowness and Lakeside (operated by Bowness Bay Boating Company and the Windermere Iron Steamship Company - though the latter does not yet operate a service to Brockhole). Don't forget that one mile walk between the boats and Ambleside, though you could catch a bus. In summer there is a pony and trap service between Waterhead and Ambleside, as long as you're not in a hurry.

By car you are handy for all parts of the Lakes - even Ullswater if you don't mind climbing up The Struggle to Kirkstone Pass (the Victorian coach and horses used to do it, though the passengers had to get out and push, hence the name of the road).

Ambleside has a one-way system which works well, in the main. The spanner in the works is the new pelican crossing in Bridge Street which cheerfully backs up traffic half-way to Grasmere on Bank Holidays (bet you think I'm joking ...). Parking in Ambleside isn't so easy if you try to get on the streets. Restricted parking and more or less limited to Compston Road and Church Street. Good pay and display car parks in Kelsick Road, Lake Road (just south of the Lakeland Sheepskin Centre). The biggest is on Rydal Road, just as you leave the village. Very handy for the shops and free during the winter (so far). Two more car parks at Waterhead, both pay and display. Don't be tempted by the wide open spaces of Charlotte Mason car park - they get very cross if visitors park there.

Tourist information centres: Waterhead (Ambleside 32729), run by the National Park, and in Church Street, Ambleside (Ambleside 32582), run by South Lakeland District Council. Both do accomodation bookings.

A rare postcard showing early Edwardian water skiers at the Low Wood Hotel , Ambleside (note: the skier is submerged as the rowing boat wasn't going fast enough).

LOWWOOD WINDERMERE.

Elterwater   C **

FLAVOUR

Situated a few miles west of Ambleside, hidden away behind Loughrigg and Silver How, at the entrance to Great Langdale. A superb setting, with the feel of a secluded country village, rather than a tourist honey pot. In reality, everyone knows about Elterwater, so it can get pretty crowded.

What you don't see from the road is one of Lakeland's more controversial features; the Langdale Timeshare, an 80 acre holiday development on the site of the old gunpowder works. The entrance is a short distance along the road into Langdale and the development itself has been very carefully screened from view. Depending who you talk to, it is either an imaginative venture which has brought much-needed prosperity into the valley, or it is a monsterous carbuncle which threatens to engulf the traditional life of Langdale. There's even a Langdale Society, formed to monitor the timeshare's growth and to try and bring the community together.

To be fair, it is a more attractive idea than emptying the village with holiday homes (like Chapel Stile, just around the corner in Great Langdale). And the development *has* been well done. Perhaps less encouraging (he said, hedging his bets) is the Timeshare's tendency to grow and swallow up old pubs like The Langdale, now tarted up and called Wainwright's (oh dear).

The village itself remains an attractive place to visit, especially on a fine summer evening. A corner shop, a village green, a nice river and some pleasant walks. The Britannia Inn, at the village centre, just by the green, is a popular meeting and drinking place for visitors and locals alike.

FACTS

Elterwater, the village, sits astride Great Langdale Beck, about half-a-mile upstream from Elterwater, the lake. The best view, from a car, is from the B5343. As you follow the road from Skelwith Bridge, you get an occassional glimpse of the lake, partly hidden by trees, you wind up the hillside, cross a cattle grid, and you suddenly come across the village lying in the valley below you. Very picturesque. To enter the village centre, turn off to the left; the main road takes you on into Great Langdale.

The village grew up around the Elterwater Gunpowder Works, which were in operation from about 1824 until the end of the First World

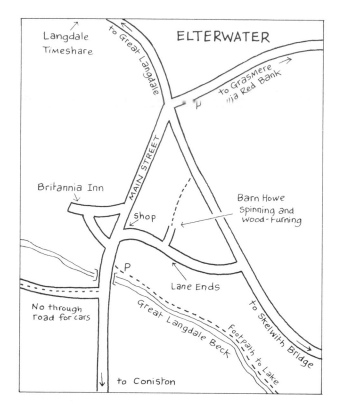

War. The other main local industry, apart from sheep farming, is the Kirkstone Slate Works, run by the Burlington Slate Company, which exports the characteristic green building slate all over the world.

THINGS TO DO

Well, apart from going for a walk or going to the pub, not a lot ...unless you fancy a jacuzzi, a game of squash, workout in a gym, or a swim? Unfortunately, for those you have to either own a timeshare chalet at the Langdales, or be resident in the Langdale Hotel. Locals can get access to the Pillar Club, but only via an annual fee. Quite an interesting commercial gallery - The Kirkstone Slate Gallery, at Skelwith Bridge (Ambleside 33296). Also a cafe.

WALKS

The whole of the Langdales to go at; Crinkle Crags, Bowfell, the Langdale Pikes; you can walk over to Grasmere, via Silver How, or even over to Borrowdale, vias Stake Pass at the head of Mickleden, but don't expect to get there and back in a day. For the less ambitious, there is a nice footpath from the car park in the village centre which takes you alongside Great Langdale Beck to Elterwater lake. A very pleasant summer evening stroll.

A good waterfall worth visiting, Skelwith Force, just behind the Skelwith Bridge Hotel, a mile or so back towards Ambleside. There's a footpath which takes you there from Elterwater, avoiding the road.

STAYING

There is always the Timeshare; they do occasionally let out chalets on a short-term basis, but in the main it is timeshare only. Ring Langdale 391 for details. They have a hotel on site, the **Langdale** (used to be called the Pillar and not to be confused with Wainwright's, which used to be called the Langdale) which operates just like any other common-or-garden upmarket hotel, with the bonus that you have access to the leisure facilities (try the steam room after you've sweated up Rosset Gill. The **Langdale Hotel** is on Langdale 302. **Britannia Inn** has accomodation, and there are a number of cottages round about which do B&B, some with evening meals.

EATING

Again, the Langdale Hotel has a licenced restaurant for non-residents (though you don't get to play in the swimming pool is you've only gone in for dinner). Good bar meals at the **Britannia**, also try the **Skelwith Bridge Hotel**. If you fancy a trip round into Little Langdale, the **Three Shires Inn** is good, both for food and accomodation.

TRANSPORT

You are more or less forced to have a car, if you want to get about from Elterwater. If you're hiking across the area, then it is fine; part of the Cumbria Way. Otherwise, you are stuck out in the wilds. One bus to Ambleside, but connections not very frequent. Contact Ribble on Ambleside 33233 for details. You could always try a mountain bike; they are for hire in the village, at Lakeland Mountain Bikes, 1 Lane Ends (Langdale 370).

Tourist information There is a National Park local information point in the village shop, Chestnut Tree Corner. For accomodation bookings, contact Ambleside or Waterhead tourist information centres.

Rydal

FLAVOUR

As a village and a place to visit, Rydal has always been overshadowed by its more famous neighbour, Grasmere. Visitors hardly give it a second glance as they hurtle past, desperate to get at Dove Cottage and cream teas. If it was not for the presence of Rydal Mount, it would probably be completely ignored. Pity, that. It is quieter than Grasmere, and its charm is a lot less 'obvious'. Although the houses are scattered, the setting for the village is very picturesque and has hardly changed since the nineteenth century.

The wooded fells rise abruptly on either side of the valley, giving exhilerating views of the lake and the surrounding mountains. It is very pleasant walking country and one route in particular - the southern shore of Rydal Water - is one of the best low level walks in Lakeland.

St. Mary's Church, from Dora's Field

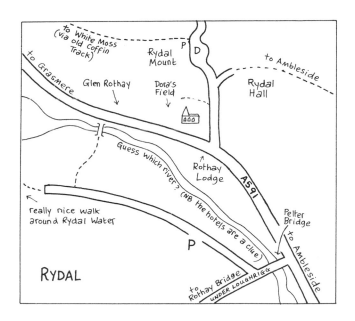

Map labels:
to White Moss (via old Coffin Track)
Rydal Mount
P D
to Ambleside
to Grasmere
Glen Rothay
Dora's Field
Rydal Hall
Guess which river? (NB the hotels are a clue)
Rothay Lodge
A591
really nice walk around Rydal Water
Pelter Bridge
to Ambleside
P
RYDAL
to Rothay Bridge UNDER LOUGHRIGG

FACTS

Rydal (the name should really be 'Rydale', meaning 'the valley where rye was grown') only just makes it as a village. It consists of a church and a few houses grouped along the narrow lane which turns off the A591, half-way between Grasmere and Ambleside. The main route between the two used to pass through what is now Rydal Park, and ran beneath Nab Scar. This was a long established packhorse route between Ambleside and Keswick and led to much of Rydal's prosperity in the sixteenth and seventeenth centuries. Until Rydal was granted the status as a parish in its own right, in 1824, coffins were carried along this route to the church at Grasmere. It is still known locally as the 'coffin track'.

Rydal Park dates from 1277 and its presence in later centuries limited the spread of the settlement.

Rydal's chief natural attraction is the small lake. Rydal Water was once known as Rothaymere - from the river which flows through from Grasmere to Ambleside. The other major attraction is Rydal Mount. This was William Wordsworth's home from 1813 until his death in 1850. When he moved here with his sister Dorothy, wife Mary and his three children, he had come up in the world since his days at Dove Cottage, though he was past his best as a poet. From here Wordsworth would issue ponderous pronouncements about the state of the nation and the art of writing poetry. He would compose angry letters to the local papers at the prospect of the new railway line to Windermere bringing hordes of uncouth visitors to his beloved Lake District (ironically, before he died he had already started to become a major tourist attraction himself). Like all his homes, it was rented rather than owned, though he did own a patch of ground just behind the church, which he originally planned to build a house for himself. He later gave this to his daughter, Dora. It is now in the hands of the National Trust and a mass of daffodils in Spring (but not *those* daffodils - they were at Gowbarrow Park, on the shores of Ullswater).

Wordsworth's great fan and sometime friend, Thomas de Quincey, owned Nab Farm (now Nab Cottage), a mile down the road towards Grasmere.

BEST BUILDINGS

Perhaps the most interesting is **Rydal Hall**, just opposite Rydal Mount. This became the family home of the Le Flemings (originally of Coniston Hall). The present building is largely 17th century, but with a Victorian front. Now owned by the Carlisle Diocese of the Church of England and used as a conference and study centre. Not open to the public but the formal gardens have recently been opened. A public footpath goes through Rydal Park to Ambleside.

St Mary's Church is only moderately interesting. Built in 1824 and had Wordsworth as church warden for a time; the Wordsworth family pew was the one in front of the lectern. One of the windows is a memorial to Thomas Arnold, headmaster of Rugby School.

Rydal Mount is not architecturally stunning (it was originally a 16th century farmhouse), but stands in attractive grounds and has a view over the valley which has hardly altered in the past two hundred years. Wordsworth rented it from the Flemings and it still remains within the Fleming family.

THINGS TO DO

Rydal Mount (Ambleside 33002) is one of the few tourist attractions in the Lake District that remains open all year round. Attractive and interesting to potter around, with some of Wordsworth's furniture and possessions on display. Some prefer it to Dove Cottage, finding it much less commercialised.

EVENTS

Rydal Sheepdog Trials, held early August in Rydal Park. Lovely setting and the number of competitors makes this one of the most atmospheric and entertaining events of its kind in Cumbria.

WALKS

The walk to Grasmere, via the old coffin track - which runs along the hillside to the north east of the A591 - is quiet and pleasant in good weather, but becomes a muddy scramble in the wet. It starts just behind Rydal Mount. There is also a good walk through to Ambleside, via a public footpath through Rydal Hall. The best walk of all - in fact, one of the nicest low level walks in the South Lakes - is along the south-west shore of Rydal Water. Cross Pelter Bridge and turn right, off the Under Loughrigg road, and follow a meandering path through the trees and over the fellside overlooking the lake. It is a couple of miles round to White Moss and Grasmere Lake. Come back either via the coffin track, or over Loughrigg.

STAYING

A limited choice in the immediate area - try the **Glen Rothay** (Ambleside 32524) or, a little nearer Grasmere, **Nab Cottage Guest House** (Grasmere 493). Best of the lot is the **Rydal Lodge Hotel** (Ambleside 33208), just opposite the turning to Rydal Mount.

EATING

Badger Bar, at the Glen Rothay, does reasonable pub food, and you can sit outside on one of those gloriously hot Lakeland summer evenings which we all know and love so well (take an umbrella).

TRANSPORT

On the main A591 bus route to Keswick, Ambleside and points beyond, so there is a bus in either direction every hour.

Parking - if visiting Wordsworth's place, there is a tiny car park up by the house, but this does tend to get rather full. The road up to Rydal Mount gets cluttered up with parked cars at the weekend. Better to park just over Pelter Bridge, there's a small National Park car park on the right, just over the cattle grid.

Tourist information   Ambleside or Grasmere.

Grasmere

FLAVOUR

Probably the Lake District's most popular village. Certainly the most famous, thanks to Wordsworth. Grasmere is what every romantic thinks a Lakeland village should be; a friendly cluster of grey, Lakeland stone houses, surrounded by mountains, set alongside a lake with a tiny island in the middle. What could be more perfect? After all, if Wordsworth came to live here, it must be good.

Well, there is no denying that Grasmere is very pretty. And it *is* right in the centre of the Lake District, and the mountains round about are magnificent. And the lake can be superb, especially early morning in late summer, with the mist rising. The trouble with idylls is that they attract too many tourists. The village centre gets fairly choked with people on summer weekends. The way to deal with this is to be more selective about when you come. The period between Easter and Spring Bank Holiday can be quiet, or try late summer, after the schools have gone back. In Autumn, the area is magnificent. Grasmere makes a good winter base, too, if you don't mind things quiet - the village practically closes down once the season is over; even the banks go on short time.

FACTS

Wandering around Grasmere valley, it is obvious that the area owed much of its early prosperity to farming, principally sheep farming. The valley was covered in woodland until the twelfth century. Thereafter, as the valley floor was cleared, the village developed as a number of widely scattered hamlets. Town End - containing Dove Cottage - and Town Head - below Helm Crag - are two settlements which have remained in a distinct group, apart from the main village.

By the fifteenth century, the valley supported ten fulling mills. These used to dress and finish Herdwick wool which was then sent to the markets at Kendal. The original mill was sited in Baneriggs wood (above the road and behind what is now Banerigg Guest House) and was built in the late thirteenth century. The wool industry declined sometime in the late sixteenth century. Agriculture has always been restricted by the geography of the valley; the valley bottom itself used to suffer from flooding. Towards the end of the last century, Manchester Corporation diverted part of Raise Beck, partly to service their new reservoir at Thirlmere and partly to help alleviate the flooding.

Today, Grasmere is almost wholly given over to the tourist indus-

St. Oswald's Church

try. It has always been popular with visitors and some of the earliest guide book writers positively eulogised. Thomas Gray visited in 1769 and went overboard: "One of the sweetest landscapes that art ever attempted to imitate ...all is peace, rusticity, and happy poverty, in its neatest and most becoming attire". The arrival of the railways at Windermere brought the first substantial influx of visitors, together with the first of the 'offcomers' - wealthy businessmen from North Lancashire who settled in the area. One of these, a Liverpool business-man called Crump, built Allan Bank, the large white house above the

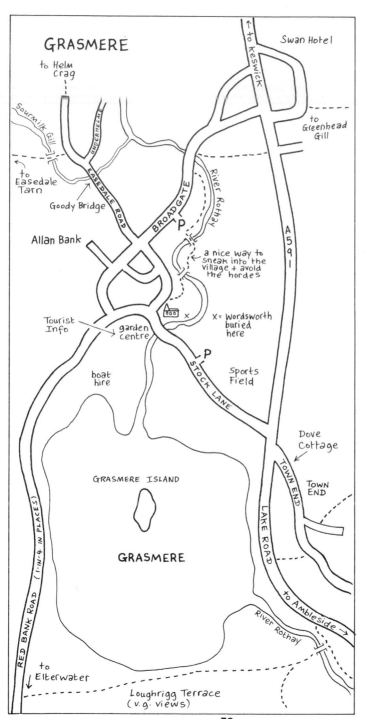

GRASMERE

to Helm Crag

Swan Hotel

to keswick

to Greenhead Gill

Sourmilk Gill

UNDERHELME

to Easedale Tarn

EASEDALE ROAD

Goody Bridge

BROADGATE

River Rothay

A591

Allan Bank

P

a nice way to sneak into the village + avoid the hordes

x = Wordsworth buried here

Tourist Info

garden centre

P

Sports Field

STOCK LANE

boat hire

Dove Cottage

TOWN END

TOWN END

GRASMERE ISLAND

LAKE ROAD

RED BANK ROAD (1-IN-4 IN PLACES)

GRASMERE

to Ambleside

River Rothay

to Elterwater

Loughrigg Terrace (v.g. views)

village. Wordsworth called it a 'temple of abomination', but it didn't stop him living there for a few years.

Wordsworth and his chums were also instrumental in preventing the railways from extending further north into Grasmere itself. Letters were written to *The Times*. Sabres were rattled. By this time, Wordsworth was less interested in the cause of the common man and more interested in preserving the valley for posh folk like himself, better able to appreciate the finer landscapes in life.

BEST BUILDINGS

St Oswald's Church is the centrepiece of the village. Parts of the church date back to the fourteenth century, and there may have been a chapel here in the eleventh century. Built, according to Wordsworth, for duration, rather than looks, it is still an interesting building with what many people ackowledge to be one of the finest church interiors in the Lakes. Oswald was the seventh century king of Northumbria and there is a site called St Oswald's Well (in the field opposite the garden centre) though the connections with Grasmere are probably apocryphal. The churchyard is famous as the site of Wordsworth's grave. He is buried here along with Dorothy, his wife Mary, daughter Dora and her husband, and his son, William. All of which makes sorting out which grave is which a shade confusing. Behind the grave is a memorial to Hartley Coleridge, the son of Samual Taylor. Wordsworth planted yews in the churchyard. There is also a memorial to him inside the church.

At the northern entrance to the churchyard is a tiny shop known as the **Grasmere Gingerbread Shop**. This was the village school, until the mid-nineteenth century. Later it became Sarah Nelson's gingerbread shop. It is still the only source for the famous gingerbread and her recipe remains a closely-guarded secret to this day.

The main road into the village dates from around 1770, the direct result of the Turnpike Act in 1745. Prior to the building of the new road, the route into Grasmere was over White Moss Common. **Dove Cottage** was once an inn, standing beside the old road. It was built in the 1600s and originally called the Dove and Olive Branch.

THINGS TO DO

Lots of gift shops. The Lakeland perfumery is a draw to some - you can try the perfumes on yourself before you buy, but don't go too mad or you'll wonder why your best friends are avoiding you when you come out. A reasonable bookshop at Dove Cottage, and Heaton Cooper (the Wainwright of the watercolours) has a gallery in the village.

Dove Cottage, Town End (Grasmere 544). Wordsworth's home from 1799 until he moved to Allan Bank in 1808. It was William and Dorothy's first home together in the Lakes since childhood. William wrote most of his best peotry here and Dorothy kept her famous journal.

Whilst they were here, William and Dorothy were inundated by guests. Coleridge was a regular visitor. Thomas de Quincey - then a young Oxford graduate - visited after three abortive attempts (he kept losing his nerve at the thought of meeting his great literary hero, and turned back at the last minute; he finally got here by offering to accompany Mrs Coleridge). Walter Scott came to stay, on one notable occasion he grew so fed up with the diet of porridge, that he developed the habit of climbing out of his bedroom window and going to the Swan Inn for a cooked breakfast. He would then sneak back into his bedroom before anyone knew he was awake. William Hazlitt and Robert Southey were other notable callers. After Wordsworth moved out, De Quincey moved in and leased the cottage for another 28 years. His most famous work, *Confessions of an English Opium-Eater*, was written whilst he lived here.

The cottage has remained pretty much as it was in Wordsworth's time. The chief guide, George Kirkby, has done wonders in getting the garden back to its original form. Apart from the first room, all the furniture in the house belonged to Wordsworth. Electric lighting is kept to a minimum and there is a refreshing absense of printed labels. During winter opening, when the fires are lit, it is possible to wander around and get a real sense of what it must have been like in Wordsworth's time. (In summer, unfortunately, the sheer pressure of visitors make the place seem very commercialised.)

Alongside the cottage is the **Grasmere and Wordsworth Museum**, a good, modern display which tells the story of Wordsworth and the Lake Poets. Combined tickets are available. Ambitious exhibitions are staged here during the summer.

Heaton Cooper Studio (Grasmere 280). Gallery devoted to paintings of famous local artist, W. Heaton Cooper. For many people, his watercolours seem to epitomise the Lake District. Originals on show; prints and greetings cards for sale.

Evenings: Grasmere Players, an amateur theatrical group, put on performances in the village hall during the summer. See tourist information centre for dates and details.

EVENTS

Grasmere Sports - Lakeland's premier traditional sporting event. Cumberland and Westmorland wrestling, races, fell running - including the Guides Race, up onto Fairfield - hound trailing, cycling. Takes over the showfield, just on the right as you enter Stock Lane. Very popular with visitors and locals alike. Get there early if you want to find parking. Held in the third Thursday after the first Monday in August. For further details, contact Grasmere 329, or the tourist information centre.

Grasmere Rushbearing - another traditional event, but going back somewhat longer. This dates from the days when church floors were covered with rush matting, the ceremony marking the changing of the rushes. Today, the ceremony consists of a procession, usually led by a band, followed by the clergy and then the children of the village, carrying rush crosses. The girls usually wear crowns, made of rushes. The procession goes round the village and ends at the church with a special rushbearing service. Grasmere rushbearing is held on the Saturday nearest St Oswald's Day (August 5th).

Wordsworth Summer Conference and **Winter School** - two events based at Dove Cottage. The Summer Conference is the more specialised of the two, attracting scholars and speakers from all over the world. The Winter School is directed more at the 'lay' enthusiast. Both are run by Richard Wordsworth, the poet's great-great-great-grandson. Details from Dove Cottage.

WALKS

Grasmere village is surrounded on all sides by Lakeland fells, so it isn't very hard to find somewhere good to walk. In ascending order of effort, try (a) Loughrigg Terrace - there are steps (of somewhat odd proportions) almost all the way up, so you have no excuse for not trying. Good view of the lake and village, (b) Easedale Tarn, a classic low-level walk from the centre of the village, following a path which takes you up alongside Sour Milk Gill to a large, hidden tarn. This was a walk which William and Dorothy loved. By continuing beyond Easedale Tarn, you could climb to (c) Sergeant Man, where you'll find yourself practically dead centre of the Lakeland fells, with a superb view across to Stickle Tarn and Pavey Ark. Come down via Greenup Edge and Far Easedale; (d) Alcock Tarn is quite good; a tough scramble up (the path is just above Dove Cottage), but come down via Greenhead Gill and you've got a magnificent view of Grasmere. Real mountaineers can continue onto Fairfield; (e) Helm Crag, another steep climb amply rewarded by the views.

STAYING

Large executive hotels abound, such as the **Wordsworth Hotel** (no, nothing to do with the poet), the **Prince of Wales**. **White Moss House** (Grasmere 295), is classier, with an excellent reputation. It stands just south of Grasmere on the A591. Some nice smaller hotels. Plenty of B&B; try **Banerigg Guest House** (Grasmere 204), small and friendly with good views over the lake.

EATING

The Rowan Tree (Grasmere 528), in Langdale Road, and **Baldry's** (Grasmere 301), in the village centre, are both good for teas and snacks. At the other end of the price scale, try **Michael's Nook** (Grasmere 496), a rather upmarket experience in the manner of Miller Howe (but not by the same people). Good vegetarian meals at the **Lancrigg Hotel** (Grasmere 528). For a real taste of Grasmere, don't forget to visit Nelson's Gingerbread shop.

TRANSPORT

Main bus route to Keswick and Ambleside, Windermere, etc. Buses every hour.

Good access north and south, though you're liable to get a bit sick of the A591. About half-an-hour's drive to Windermere, ditto to Keswick. See Ambleside for other warnings. Reasonable parking in the

A gang of international gastronomic criminals, about to attempt to steal the recipe for Sara Nelson's celebrated gingerbread

village. Car parks in Stock Lane and just north of the village centre in Broadgate. Both pay and display. Parking on the main street is effectively nil, though there is space for half-a-dozen cars round by the village green. There always seem to be large numbers of people meandering aimlessly in the middle of the road in Grasmere, so drive carefully.

Tourist information National Park information centre just behind the garden centre, opposite the church. Telephone Grasmere 245.

Highgate, Kendal

Chapter 3

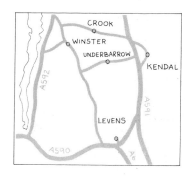

Kendal

Kendal

FLAVOUR

Kendal was the largest town in the old county of Westmorland (though not the capital - that was Appleby). Now that we're all in Cumbria, that position has been usurped by Carlisle. Kendal is an attractive, historical town, still the centre for a great deal of local industry, including K Shoes and Provincial Insurance. It fairly bustles with activity on market days. In recent years, a lot of the charm has been diminished by traffic problems, exacerbated by shops closing, changing hands and remaining empty. The advent of the new Stricklandgate shopping development has also led to turmoil. But there are a lot of pleasant places in Kendal, if you take the trouble to seek them out.

Known as the 'auld grey town' - the whole place looks as though it has been carved from limestone - Kendal stands less than a mile outside the National Park boundary. Just far enough to be overlooked by the majority of people hurtling towards Grasmere and so forth ... This means that the town has retained much of its old character. As a shopping centre, it continues to flourish, never having succumbed to the onslaught of gift shops and Lakeland wool shops that have hit the other main centres.

FACTS

Kendal is terribly historical. The Romans built a fort just south of the present centre, at Watercrook. *Alauna* was protected on three sides by the river and situated at a good fording point. The other main fording point, farther north, was the site of an Anglo-Saxon settlement. In the eighth century, they put up a cross and, a little later, a small church. It was mentioned in the Domesday book. The medieval township grew up around this church and later became Kirkland, predating the development of Kendal itself.

Kendal grew to become one of the main manufacturing towns of pre-industrial England. Between the thirteenth and nineteenth centuries, there were more than thirty mills on the River Kent - for sawing, milling, papermaking, bobbin-making. But Kendal was first and foremost a centre for the wool industry (the town motto is "wool is my bread").

The wool trade began around the thirteenth century; Kendal was a natural centre for the farmers and traders in the surrounding countryside. A market charter had been granted as long ago as 1189, making it the first in Cumbria. There were once up to sixty inns in the town to accomodate the travellers and tradespeople. Some of the wool was even exported to the continent during the fourteenth and fifteenth centuries. Kendal was also famous for a type of cloth known as 'Kendal Green', which got a mention by Shakespeare in *Henry IV*.

The castle which stands on the hill to the east of the Kent was built around 1180, by Gilbert FitzReinfred and his wife, Helewise de Lancaster. In 1391, it became the property of Sir William del Parre, whose great great great grand-daughter was Katherine Parr, Henry VIII's sixth wife. But did you also know that Kendal has another, much earlier castle? Read on ...

BEST BUILDINGS

Kendal has so many nice and interesting old buildings, it is difficult to know where to start. How about with a building which isn't there anymore. Kendal's first castle was a wooden stockade affair - a motte and bailey castle - built in 1092, by Ketel de Tailbois, the third Baron of Kendal. His grandfather, the first baron, came over with William the Conqueror. It stood in a commanding position on a hill to the west of the river. It was abandoned after a hundred years or so when the owners decided to move across the river and build a real castle, out of stone. They were obviously going up in the world. The site of Kendal's first castle is up Beast Banks; walk a few hundred yards up the road until you come to a little alleyway on your left called Garth Heads. Turn along there until you come to some steps on your right. These lead you onto a large, flat bowling green. This was once the bailey. The castle stood on the knoll in front of you. The obelisk which now stands there commemorates the Revolution of 1688.

The **stone castle** is now a ruin, but worth exploring, with brilliant views over town and the surrounding countryside.

The parish church, **Holy Trinity**, in Kirkland, is mostly eighteenth century, but stands on the site of the original Anglo-Saxon church. In fact, part of the eighth century cross can be seen inside (along with Katherine Parr's prayer book). Just outside the church grounds, is

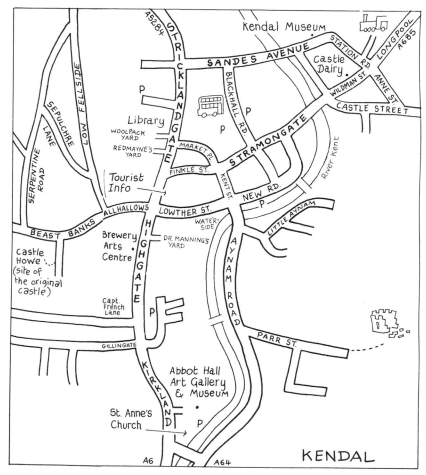

Abbot Hall, built as a private house for Colonel George Wilson in 1759. It stands in a very attractive position beside the river.

    Kirkland is the most attractive part of Kendal, but there are some other places worth seeking out and Kirkland makes a good start for a town trail. Just beyond the church is the **Ring O'Bells** pub, which dates back to 1741. Still very small and cosy inside. As you head up **Highgate**, Kendal's most distinctive architectural feature is not very apparent. This is the presence of the 'yards'. There are tiny alleys and courtyards which open off the main street, usually with tiny, restricted entrances. One popular theory is that they were built like this for defensive reasons, to hold off the Scots during the marauding season. Unfortunately, the real explanation is a more prosiac; the yards were built centuries after the Scottish border raids, during the late 1700s. They were built to house workers in the weaving industry - the cramped style was simply to cram as many people into as small a space as possible.

There were once about 150 yards in Kendal. Often they were named after the owner of the main house, which usually stood at the top of the yard. Look out for **Yard 83**, Dr Manning's Yard, on the righthand side as you walk up Highgate. The yards on this side of Highgate used to run in parallel lines down to the river, where there were factories, weaving shops, dying works, even a windmill, at one point (hence the name of Yard 65 - Windmill Yard).

Farther up the street, is the **Fleece Inn**, built about 1656. The sign on the side shows the coat of arms - wool hooks and teasles. Just next to the Fleece is the **Old Shambles**, where the butchers used to work (hence Beast Banks, just behind). The area behind this part of Kendal, Fellside, used to be the poor area; a mass of crammed houses, tiny streets and tenements. Most of it has now been replaced by modern housing, but some of the original names remain (Sepulchre Lane is a nice one).

The **Titus Wilson** shop front is very pretty. The building itself is under redevelopment, but let's hope the shop survives. Beyond the Fleece, is the **White Hart Inn**, one of Kendal's early coaching inns. Cross the main road and you enter Market Place. Half-way down, on your right, is **New Shambles**, a nice, cobbled alley, rather like its namesake in York, only much smaller. Three guesses why the street slopes in such a charming and picturesque way: it was designed to allow blood and offal from the butchers' shops to flow down towards the river. Bet you wish you hadn't asked now.

A couple of other things to look out for in Kendal; opposite the

The early days of Kendal's one-way system (nb the wagon is going the WRONG WAY).

library is Thomson and Matthews estate agent. Above their shop front is a hog. This used to advertise a brush manufacturer. Finally, in Lowther Street, see if you can spot the Turk. He stands fifteen feet off the pavement and was another trade sign, this time for Gawith Hoggarth & Co., snuff and tobacco manufacturers. The original sign was erected in 1873, though the present one is a replica.

THINGS TO DO

Reasonable open-air market on Wednesdays and Saturdays. Plenty of shops, especially clothing. Usual department stores. One or two nice 'curiosities' and some good antique shops.

Abbot Hall Art Gallery, Kirkland (Kendal 22464). Excellent art gallery set in an attractive Georgian mansion in parkland beside the river. Not the tiny provincial gallery you might expect but one of the best in the country.

Museum of Lakeland Life and Industry - an extension of Abbot Hall, housed in the stable blocks, though a separate enterprise in its own right(joint tickets are available). Excellent displays, with plenty of farming and craft machinery and tools - none of it under glass cases, so you can prowl around and peer under things as much as you wish. A fine farming museum in a separate little gallery and a superb replica of a nineteenth century street scene. Good craft shop, too.

Kendal Museum, Station Road (Kendal 21374). One of the country's oldest museums and now under the wing of Abbot Hall. Good diaramas enabling you to stroll back into Westmorland's prehistory. Also features a World Wildlife Gallery which has nothing to do with the Lake District, but a lot to do with the history of Kendal Museum.

Castle Dairy, Wildman Street (Kendal 21170). One of Kendal's oldest buildings. Not a lot to see except for the building itself, but very cheap to get in.

Kendal Heritage Centre, Stricklandgate Shopping Centre. Displays and background to Kendal's early history, based on the archeological remains found when work on the site of the shopping centre first began, in 1986.

South Lakeland Leisure Centre, Burton Road (Kendal 29511). Large new leisure centre with swimming pool, squash, badminton, weight training and vasrious regular club activities.

Evenings: Occasional talks and concerts at Abbot Hall. Also concerts at the Parish Church in Kirkland. The Leisure Centre features The Westmorland Hall, a venue for concerts and performances of all kinds (note that it has a separate number to the sports facility - Kendal 29702).

Brewery Arts Centre, Highgate (Kendal 25133). Set in a restored brewery, with a recent extension at the back of the new YHA building. The hub of Kendal's cultural life, there's usually a lot going on here. Plays, mime theatre, folk, jazz and rock concerts, workshops - even films. Kendal's main cinema closed down in 1986 but now the Brewery has decided to step into the breach and develop facilities to show Real Films. The Brewery also holds regular arts and photographic exhibitions in their new Warehouse Gallery, which are open during the day. At weekends during the summer they hold regular family days, with events designed to keep kids and harassed parents amused. Cafe is a good place to go to catch up on local activities.

EVENTS

The Brewery Arts Centre sponsors two music festivals each year, with performances at both the Brewery and the Leisure Centre: Kendal Jazz Festival, held around the end of summer, and Kendal Folk Festival, in late August. Well-known names frequently feature at both.

Kendal Gathering - a two and a half week event which occurs late August/early September. A mini-festival with a lot of contrasting events going on throughout Kendal, including shows, concerts, contests, exhibitions, dances and culminating with the Torchlight Procession, a sort of late evening fancy dress parade through the main streets. For details contact Kndal 20040 or the tourist information centre.

Westmorland County Show - held the second Thursday in September at the County Showfield, just outside town. A good one-day event with agricultural displays and competitions, Sumberland and Westmorland wrestling, show jumping, horse drawn carriage driving. Usually scheduled to coincide with the Kendal Gathering. One of Cumbria's best agricultural shows. For details, contact Kendal 23479 or the tourist information centre.

Lakeland Rose Show - held the second weekend in July on the County Showfield. A showcase for horticulturalists all over the country, with lots to see apart from the plants; car shows, massed bands, parachute displays. One of Cumbria's most vaunted events. Used to be held at Holker Hall but recently transfered to Kendal. Details on Kendal 23855.

WALKS

Kendal is not particularly handy for getting out into the open country-side by foot; some nice walks around if you've access to public transport or a car.

The walk up to Kendal Castle is nice, if short. Very pleasant to stand by the ruined walls and look back over the town or out to the Lakes. Alternatively, if you head up Gillingate and follow the Brigsteer Road for a mile or so - until it crosses the bridge over the A591 - it is possible to strike out towards Scout Scar and magnificent views across the Lyth Valley.

A short drive out to Natland and there's a good walk across the fields by the River Kent to reach the site of the old Roman fort at Watercrook. Or head the opposite direction and follow the river south to Sedgwick and cross the rickety little bridge to reach Sizergh Castle (via a lane which goes under the A591). Whitbarrow Scar is only a few miles to the south west of Kendal, on the other side of the Lyth Valley; another limestone escarpment with pleasant walks if you can't be bothered to head for the fells.

STAYING

Not bad at all for accomodation. For a start, being slightly outside the National Park means that accomodation will be easier to find, especially at bank holidays; places inside the magic boundary always fill up first. To get to Grasmere, Coniston and the central Lakes, you're a bit out of the way, but you do have optional routes to the north, enabling you to get to Keswick via the A6 or the M6. If you can't face the crowds in mid-summer, you can always head east for the day and explore the Eden Valley or the Pennines.

Not a huge number of B&B in the town itself, but a number scattered about in the surrounding villages. Hotels are to be found on the outskirts, rather than in the town centre, though there are some good 'pub'-type hotels. Outside, try the **Gateway Hotel** (Kendal 24187), the **Crooklands Hotel** (Crooklands 432 - and very handy for the motor-way), or for something a bit more homely and special, **Greenriggs** (Crosthwaite 387) at Underbarrow.

EATING

Hm... Surprisingly, not as good for good, upmarket restaurants as Win-dermere or Ambleside. **The Moon** (Kendal 29254) in Highgate (oppo-site the Brewery Arts Centre), is excellent and there is a good Indian restaurant, Mogul E Azan (Kendal 24074), in Wildman Street. Where Kendal really scores is for nice cafes and tea shops: **Farrer's Coffee**

Shop, Stricklandgate; **Waterside Wholefoods**, (down by the river); **Nutter's Eating House**, Yard 11, Stramongate; all are good, with busy, friendly atmospheres. All serve lunches. The **Brewery Arts Centre** has a restaurant - a bit college-like but good value.

TRANSPORT

Fine for rail connections, though Kendal station is (a) not the mainline station, that's at Oxenholme, a couple of miles south; (b) on the other side of town from all the shops and a good twenty-minute walk from the Town Hall; (c) a dump - not an inviting prospect at all, though the Lakes Line Action Group have their sights set firmly on encouraging British Rail to do something about it, following their successful heckling over Windermere. For train times, ring Oxenholme (Kendal 20397).

Kendal is well-served for buses - in fact, following deregulation there are a number of bus companies fighting it out to sweep up all the passengers. Buses every hour into the Lakes, and down to Lancaster. The bus station used to be in Blackhall Road, but at the time of writing had been demolished to make way for the large shopping development. Presumably something will take its place. Buses also stop outside the Town Hall, though these are often local services in and around the residential areas of town.

If you are travelling by car, steel yourself to encounter Kendal's diabolical one-way system. Enter from the Windermere end and it is like leaping onto a merry-go-round. You orbit the town, cross the river and crawl back up the main streets, with no apparent sign of car parks, circling hopelessly until you run out of petrol or suffer apoplexy. If coming to town for the first time, you really need an eagle-eyed navigator, capable of divining car parks on the flimsiest of clues. Parking on the main streets is nil. There is restricted parking on a few roads such as Beast Banks (up at the top can be quite useful, if you don't mind the steep trek back up the car). Car parks exist in Blackhall Road, by the river in New Road (though not much chance of getting in *there* after 10.00 a.m.) and by the Parish Church in Kirkland (not in Abbot Hall, please). There is also a limited amount of parking at The Brewery Arts Centre. The last two are probably the best bet.

Tourist information   In the Town Hall, telephone Kendal 25758.

Market days   Wednesday and Saturday   Early closing Thursday

Winster

Winster is not a 'touristy' sort of village, yet a lot of visitors to the area seem to know about it. Ask most people for their impression and it is the little whitewashed post office which springs to mind. No longer a post office, alas, it is now a private house and stands in the centre of the village, on the left as you travel through from Bowness. The building is dated 1600.

Winster is a very attractive little village. Saved from being too twee by the presence of a working farm. There is a pub, the Brown Horse Inn, which looks old an attractive from the outside, but somehow never seems to quite live up to its promise. Down the road opposite is **Holy Trinity** church in a lovely setting among the trees.

Busy high street at Winster

Crook

$\mathbb{C}$ *

The village of Crook lies on the B5284, a fairly quiet country road between Bowness and Kendal. Approach from the Bowness direction and you pass a sign for the village. You carry on and after a while begin to wonder what has happened to the village. There's no sign of it. In fact, Crook is strung out very thin along the road. It does not have a centre as such. The point most people would identify as the centre is the pub, the Sun Inn. There are a few more farms and houses scattered along the road behind the pub. The church, a fairly plain affair dedicated to St Catherine, is almost a mile back along the road to Bowness.

Not really a village to savour. It can be the object of some reasonable walks - there are several footpaths across the fields from Staveley and Underbarrow. Makes a good base to stay if you want to be off the beaten track in quiet, unspoilt countryside.

A couple of architectural points of interest: the tower of the old church, built around the mid-seventeenth century, is still visible, on a hill just south west of the current church. You can get to it via a public footpath. Crook also has a fifteenth century pele tower, now attached to Hollin Hall farmhouse, just off the narrow road from Crook to Staveley.

Underbarrow

$\mathbb{C}$ *

Underbarrow is one of a number of small villages dotted about on the maze of minor roads at the back of Cartmel Fell. Try to get there by night and you spend half your time parked beside the road going over your map with a torch. It takes its name from the fact that it sits below Helsington Barrows, the bluff limestone escarpment to the east. (Good view of the whole valley from Scout Scar.) Famous for its pub, The Punch Bowl (a popular name for pubs round here - there's another just down the road at Crosthwaite). Edward Burrough, the Quaker and one of George Fox's early converts was born at Underbarrow. According to Nikolaus Pevsner the church is of a "naughty design", but it looked perfectly well-behaved to me. Nice countryside but otherwise not a lot to see.

There is a good hotel nearby, **Greenriggs** (Crosthwaite 387), which is small and pleasant. **Tullythwaite House** (Crosthwaite 397) is excellent for farmhouse teas - but ring first to check times.

Levens

Levens is a quiet residential village on a hillside, overlooking fields and the A590. Of moderate size, it has a couple of shops, some nice views of the southern fells and a pleasant church. Otherwise, not a lot for the general visitor. The majority of the houses are modern and the impression is a bit like walking around a housing estate, hemmed in with drystone walls.

St. John's Church occupies a position overlooking the Lythe Valley. As usual, the graveyard gets one of the best views in the village. Go round to the back oif the church and there are three cast-iron bells, hanging in a low, slate-roofed shelter. These were brought from Milnethorpe in 1913 and enable the parishoners to boast that their church doesn't disturb the neighbours - the bells have no clappers.

The church was built in 1829, commissioned by Mary Howard of Levens Hall. The interior is plain but on rather a grand scale.

STAYING & EATING

Just below the church is the **Hare and Hounds Inn** (Sedgwick 60408), which has accomodation and provides bar meals. An alternative is **The Wheatsheaf** (Crosthwaite 254) at Brigsteer.

This part of South Lakeland remains fairly quiet throughout the summer and is a good place to head for if you're here for a weekend and not too bothered about getting up to the northern fells. Very handy for the motorway, if you're coming from the south - junction 36 is about twenty minutes away.

THINGS TO DO

Levens is most famous for **Levens Hall**, a fine Elizabethan mansion which stands in magnificent grounds a short distance south of Levens Bridge. The hall is renouned for its Topiary Gardens. A fascinating place to visit, with events held throughout the season to attract families. Telephone Sedgwick 60321.

Head the opposite way from Levens, towards Kendal, and you come to **Sizergh Castle**. This is the family home of the Stricklands and began life as a pele tower, built in 1340. It is the largest tower in Cumbria still standing. Very attractive grounds and some fine furniture and carvings inside the house. It is run by the National Trust, details on Sedgwick 60285.

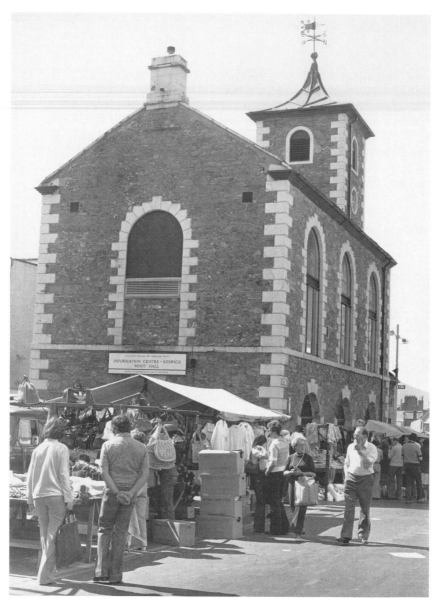

The Moot Hall and Market at Keswick

Chapter 4

Keswick

Keswick   𝔹 **

FLAVOUR

Keswick has a sort of multiple personality. Depending whether you live there, or what time of year you visit, you could go away with any one of three entirely conflicting views of the town.

Come in winter and the main street will impress you with its dignified, eighteenth century, stone-built houses, its rugged charm and its superb setting among the high fells of Lakeland. You might be lucky enough to catch its bustling market or arrive on a sunny winter day and look over the rooftops and see Skiddaw in the distance, lightly frosted with snow.

Alternatively, you could end up here in the middle of a hot, sticky summer afternoon, find the street thronged with cars and pedestrians, the shop fronts a mass of postcards, gifts and noddy rucksacs. If the market is on, you won't be able to park. The one way system and the narrow streets will drive you up the wall and the hunt for somewhere decent to get a tea and will leave you parched and exhausted.

Again, if you live here, Keswick is a town with sprawling modern estates contrasting with snooty Victorian houses, all jostling with each other for the best view of the lake and fells, and trying desperately hard to remain aloof from the tourists.

In other words, it is the sort of place you avoid in summer and sneak back to savour when the crowds have gone.

Keswick is the northern Bowness. Whereas the latter is flooded by coach parties from Manchester and the North-West, in Keswick they pour in from Newcastle and all points North-East. But it is a curious mixture; because of the architecture and the location, the place has a dignity and an old fashioned air which is at odds with the tourist shops and the crowds and traffic.

Real fellwalkers use Keswick, not just the general tourist. Some of

71

these are just passing through, on their way to or from Borrowdale, but many will be using the town as a base for Cat Bells or Skiddaw.

Keswick has its own uniform where the great outdoors is concerned. In Ambleside, it is all high-tech, up to the minute stuff. In Windermere, you can get away with posing around in Rohan gear. In Keswick, the *de rigour* outfit consists of battered Barbour jacket, tweed walking breeks, Aran sweater and heavy leather walking boots. The adventurous ones may substitute an approved Forestry Commission-green cagoule for the Barbour jacket. Rucksac, if carried, should on no account be one of these brightly-coloured, anatomically designed climbers' sacs, but should be dung brown, preferably with a metal frame, and be as uncomfortable as possible. Optional extras include a walking stick (preferably chewed by a dog before use) and a flat cap. There, now you know how to blend in. (In Grasmere, in case you were wondering, you should wear a plastic transparent raincoat, crimpelene trousers and a tartan cap with a lump of Scots heather stuck in it.)

FACTS

The original settlement was at Great Crosthwaite, between the present town centre and the A66. There does not seem to have been a Roman encampment of any kind at Keswick, though its location would have made it an ideal spot and there is some evidence to suggest a road ran through here from the Roman fort at Castlesteads to the fort at Papcastle, near Cockermouth.

The original church at Crosthwaite was built 553 A.D., and named after St Kentigern (or St Mungo, as he is sometimes known) the sixth century Bishop of Glasgow. He set up a cross here, giving rise to the name 'Crosfeld' or Crosthwaite - meaning 'the cross in the clearing'. In 1198, Richard I gave the church to Fountains Abbey, which farmed the area for three hundred years. Keswick was granted a market charter in the thirteenth century and with the dissolution of the Abbey in the sixteenth century, wool produced in Borrowdale went to Keswick, rather than to the Abbey itself, thereby increasing its importance as a market town.

Industry hit the area in 1565, the year after Queen Elizabeth had formed the Company of the Mines Royal to "search, dig, try, roast and melt all manner of mines and ores of gold, silver, copper and quicksilver". On 1st of April, 1565, Goldscope Mine was opened in the Newlands Valley to dig for copper ore. Fifty German miners were brought over to lend their expertise. (Goldscope is a corruption of the German name for the mine, which meant 'God's Gift'.) The German miners established themselves on Derwent Island - possibly to distance themselves from antagonism from the locals, though this was later overcome as, by 1567, fourteen of the miners were married to local girls.

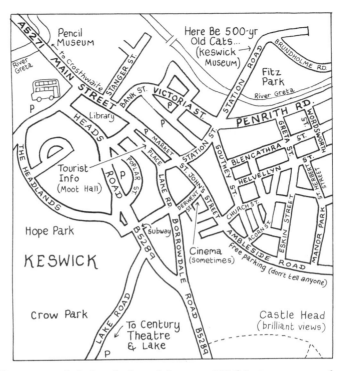

Keswick became a thriving industrial town. Within two years of the opening of Goldscope, there were six furnaces in the area, supplied with ore from Newlands and Caldbeck. In the next 150 years, huge tracts of woodland went to provide charcoal for the furnaces. The mining of copper in the Keswick area ceased in the mid-seventeenth century, but by then it had begun to be superceded by the 'wad' mines; graphite, dug from the fells above Seathwaite. This was a valuable resource, used for a variety of purposes, from casting cannon balls, glazing pottery, even as a cure for "cholick". At some point, a bright spark realised you could even draw with the stuff, and so was born the Cumberland pencil industry, home of the world's first pencils.

The romantic age of tourism began in the late eighteenth century and Keswick was a popular resort, described as consisting of "three circumstances, beauty, horror and immensity united". Derwent Island was bought in 1778 by an eccentric bachelor named Joseph Pocklington, who built a house, some follies and a stone circle, to 'enhance' its picturesque splendour.

Keswick has a number of notable literary associations; Coleridge and Southey once lived in Greta Hall, the pleasant mansion house next to the river and now part of Keswick school. Coleridge used to walk from here to visit Wordsworth, when the latter lived at Grasmere.

Southey lived here for forty years, until his death in 1843. John Ruskin visited Friar's Crag as a boy - there is a memorial to him, overlooking the lake. And one of the vicars of Crosthwaite church was Canon Rawnsley, a co-founder of the National Trust.

In 1864 the railway arrived, in the form of the line from Penrith to Cockermouth. The Keswick Hotel sprang up and the development of the present town began.

BEST BUILDINGS

The centre of Keswick is predominantly Victorian. Even the **Moot Hall** dates from 1813, though it stands on the site of the original market hall. It was built using materials from the ruins of a mansion on Lords Island. The ground floor used to have open archways and housed a small market. The National Park established an information centre in the hall, in 1971. The bell tower is fun; the clock has only one hand and the bell inside is dated 1601. Keswick, like Kendal, has a number of Yards, the **Pack Horse Yard** remaining the best example. This is still a pleasant shopping area, though currently under threat of development.

Lake Road seems to have become some sort of centre for mountaineering shops, though I'm not sure why. On the corner is the massive and slightly crumbling edifice of **Fisher's**; a long-established shop, specialising in a vast range of outdoor gear, from plastic raincoats to ice axes and crampons. The most notable feature is the vast painting of a climber, above the main entrance. Hope they don't update it to give him a Gore-tex cag and plastic mountain boots ...

St Kentigern's Church at Crosthwaite, is well worth seeking out. Although parts of some twelfth century foundations and a fourteenth century wall remain, the church is now a mixture of styles, the result of alterations in the seventeenth and nineteenth centuries. Inside there is a memorial to Robert Southey.

Finally, on the hill a mile east of the town centre, is one of England's most spectacularly-site Neolithic monuments, **Castlerigg Stone Circle**. This circle of 48 standing stones, 90 feet across, dates from around 2,000 B.C. Its setting would have been ideal for a religeous monument of some kind, though its real purpose remains a mystery. (For the record, the author suspects it could well have been the result of a prehistoric YTS scheme.)

THINGS TO DO

Keswick Museum, Fitz Park (Keswick 73263). Situated just outside the town centre; sometimes also referred to as the Fitzpark Museum. Compared to Lakeland's other thrusting, dynamic, modern heritage interpretative centres, the Keswick Museum is decidedly ramshackle and old-fashioned. But therein lies its charm. Instead of interactive videos and the latest in high-tech interpretative displays telling you all sorts of things you hadn't really wanted to know, in the Keswick Museum you find out for yourself. That means prowling around, trying to read badly-lit labels, peering into darkened corners and lifting off covers to see what's underneath. Well worth it, though. Where else could you expect to find a 500-year old cat, a set of musical slates played before Queen Victoria, the original copy of The Three Bears (before Goldilocks got into the act) and a collection of letters from, by and to the Lake Poets?

Cumberland Pencil Museum, Southey Works (Keswick 72116). Now part of the Rexel Pencil Factory. Fascinating little museum for children of all ages; exhibits, videos, the world's largest pencil (it's in the Guiness Book of Records); everything you wanted to know about pencils but were afraid to ask.

Lingholme Gardens, Portinscale (Keswick 72003). Very pleasant combination of formal and natural gardens with magnificent woodland and views across the lake to Borrowdale. One of the best ways of getting there is by boat, disembarking at Low Brandlehow.

Keswick Spa, Station Road (Keswick 72760). Well, they said they were going to redevelop the old station area, but somehow one didn't quite expect this. Resembling one of those pressurised domes that fifties science fiction authors used to dot all over the moon, Keswick Spa is billed as an indoor 'resort'. It contains a swimming pool, water slide, cafe, shop, restaurant and a constant temperature of eighty-five degrees Farenheit. Even low-voltage space invader machines, so you don't get a shock, straight out of the pool. Doesn't seem quite couth for the Lake District, somehow, but popular on wet days - and especially recommended for families with young kiddies.

Derwentwater Launches (Keswick 72263 or 73013) are more entertainment than transport. Launches run circuits of Derwentwater at regular intervals throughout the day in the summer season. They take it in turns to run clockwise and counterclockwise around the lake, and there are a number of getting off points, making it possible to get off, walk between

THE classic view of Keswick, by the Abraham brothers

landing stages and catch the boat back to Keswick. Good way to see the surrounding fells.

Also within striking distance are **Mirehouse**, a delightful English country manor house (see Bassenthwaite); and **Whinlatter Visitor Centre**, on the Whinlatter Pass road (Braithwaite 469), a Forestry Commission centre, with walks, trails and exhibitions.

Evenings: **Alhambra Cinema**, St John's Street (Keswick 72195). Rather small and closes in winter.

Century Theatre, Lakeside Car Park (Keswick 74411). Yes, that's right - that chaotic-looking collection of blue portacabins really does house a theatre, and a rather fine one at that. The surroundings might not be all the players deserve, but it does make a memorable evening of your visit. Eventually, there will be a permanent construction. The theatre is open throughout the summer months and the resident company performs three plays in rotation, usually two or three days at a time, so if you're here for a week you could see all three. Usually something classical, something comic and something modern. The Keswick tourist information centre has full details of the summer programme and can make bookings.

Incidentally, try visiting the **Twa Dogs Inn**, Penrith Road (Keswick 72599) for sight of a local curiosity - the Boggart, a cross between a fox and a badger. Very rare.

EVENTS

The **Keswick Show** is held annually, on August Bank Holiday Monday. **Keswick Convention** is a famous religious gathering held two weeks in mid-July. The town has to be seen to be believed; packed with stalls, all selling bibles. Finally, at Threlkeld there are annual **Sheepdog Trials**, held in mid-August.

WALKS

You are spoilt for choice in Keswick. From the town centre, walk down to the boat landings and along to Friar's Crag. This is a very pleasant little stroll and you can extend it as far as you want along the shore, walking the footpath across open fields. In fact, if you are keen you can do a complete circuit of the lake, all seven miles. If you only want to do the best bits, explore Friar's Crag and then return to the boat landing and take the launch to Manesty Woods. Follow the lovely, wooded shore-line round to Hawes End and catch a launch back to Keswick.

Hawes End makes a good starting point for the ascent of Cat Bells, the long, low summit which lies alongside the western shore of Derwen-twater. Quite a steep climb and you need to allow two or three hours for this, depending how fit you are. Be warned: more accidents happen on Cat Bells than any other fell. It isn't any more trecherous than the others, but it looks too easy. Treat it with respect. Take waterproofs and wear decent shoes or boots.

The National Park have recently renovated part of the old Keswick to Penrith railway line, turning it into a walking track. Worth exploring. Details available in a National Park walks leaflet from the tourist information centre.

Finally, a magnificent viewpoint which shouldn't be missed. Castlehead is the wooded knoll almost due east of Friar's Crag. It can be reached from the Borrowdale road, a footpath leading up through the trees to a superb view of Derwentwater.

STAYING

Bet you didn't know that Keswick has more B&Bs than any town of its size anywhere in the country. You did? You must have cheated and looked in *The Good Guide*. Accomodation in the lower price ranges no problem. Higher up the scale, not so much in the way of classy, upmarket hotels - Keswick seems to go in for the large and impersonal, as a rule. But try the **Keswick Hotel**, Station Road (Keswick 72020) or the **Underscar Hotel**, just outside Keswick (Keswick 72469). Leave the immediate environs of the town and things look up. Try the **Red House Hotel** at Underskiddaw (Keswick 72211) or the **Ravenstone Hotel**, half-way along Bassenthwaite on the A591 (Bassenthwaite Lake 240).

Keswick is brilliant for access to the northern fells, anywhere in Borrowdale or down to Ullswater (sneak down via the A5091, through Dockray). Also well-placed for exploring the quieter countryside just outside the National Park, to the north.

EATING

Not so brilliant. A real dearth of high class restaurants, though things are improving. Try the **Old Station Restaurant**, Station Raod (Keswick 72545). Good meals and snacks at **Maysons**, Lake Road (Keswick 74104) or **Archway Antiques**, St John's Street (Keswick 72842). Good pub meals at the **Dog and Gun**, Lake Road.

TRANSPORT

Still part of the main bus route through the Lakes, up the A591, so good hourly connections to Ambleside (connections to Coniston, Hawkshead) and Windermere (connections to Kendal and Lancaster). Also good for Carlisle, reasonable for Penrith and okay for Borrowdale. Bus connections connect up with Penrith railway station, if you're coming up to the lakes by train. There's a regular bus service from Keswick to Seatoller, via Rosthwaite. The Mountain Goat runs a service to Buttermere, via Stair (Keswick 73962).

Handy for all parts by car, though rather a trek to the southern lakes (about an hour to Windermere via the A591). If you want to go out to Ravenglass, a good tip is to go out via Wrynose and Hardknott Pass, come back via the country lanes on the western fringes of the Lakes, through Calder Bridge and Loweswater village, then back over the Newlands Pass. Keswick is very handy for the M6 - about half an hour from junction 40 at Penrith.

There is restricted parking on all the main streets. Limited parking in Market Square, except when the market is on. The car parks are all pay-and-display. The central one, off Victoria Street, fills up very quickly in summer. Another one in Heads Road, or try round by the bus station. The best car park is down by the lake. It's only a five minute walk back into town. Keswick can get very congested with traffic, so use the bypass if you're heading through, or get there early.

Tourist information National Park information centre in the Moot Hall, telephone Keswick 72803. For accomodation bookings and winter info, Keswick 72645.

Market day Saturday, early closing Wednesday.

Grange-in-Borrowdale ℂ **

Originally a farm, or 'grange', belonging to Furness Abbey. In the thirteenth century it was a large sheep farm, one of a number scattered about the region run by the Cistercian monks. The village is now a popular spot for 'off-comers' to the area. For the car driver, the first impression is the graceful, double-arched bridge which takes you across the River Derwent and into the village. The river here is quite shallow and gentle, and a popular spot for paddling in summer. The village itself is very attractive, with pleasant, local stone cottages and farm-houses. The newer houses give it the air of a dormitory village.

Just south of Grange is a famous Lakeland oddity, the **Bowder Stone**. A 30' high, 60' long boulder, standing on one edge in a clearing. It looks as if it might topple over at any minute, but in fact it's been here since the last Ice Age. It was a great hit with the Victorians and has been a popular tourist attraction ever since. There's a ladder against the side, so you can scramble all over it. You can even shake hands underneath it, if you're feeling brave. There is a small car park nearby, but you have to look out for it.

Grange-in-Borrowdale, another view by the Abraham brothers

Rosthwaite

In summer, if you leave Keswick and decide to go exploring, south, into Borrowdale Valley, you will find yourself joining a stream of cars, following the narrow, winding road which threads the valley. Seeing the best of the area can be difficult from a car, you're constantly having to crane out of the windows to see the high, valley walls which tower above the road. At some points, the sides of the valley close right in. The first of these, at the point by Castle Crag, was known to the early guide book writers as the 'Jaws of Borrowdale'. High, tree-lined crags rise up on either side. Alongside the road runs the river Derwent, but there is precious little room for anything else.

Once through the Jaws and into the valley proper, it opens out again and you come to the first of a number of settlements, Rosthwaite.

Walkers in Borrowdale, thinking that they can cheat by using the road ...

This tiny village is solid and businesslike. Not picturesque in itself, but with a backdrop like this anything looks good. The main part of the village lies off the main road, to the west.

A very popular spot with walkers, the car park (just along the road opposite the post office) makes a natural starting point for expeditions onto Watendlath Fell, to Castle Crag or to Dale Head. The river, which runs behind the Royal Oak Hotel, is very pleasant and there's a nice walk along the old road, on the east side of Stonethwaite Beck. Head the opposite way, and there's some lovely wooded countryside around the river, heading towards Castle Crag.

Castle Crag itself, half-a-mile north of the village, was once an ancient British hill fort. It commands a superb view of the valley. On its flanks is abundant evidence of the slate quarrying which used to take place around here.

The **Royal Oak Hotel** (Borrowdale 214) is good for bar meals, and the **Scafell Hotel** (Borrowdale 208) is a pleasant base if you're staying in the area. Also try the **Hazel Bank Hotel** (Borrowdale 248) - the fictional home of Rogue Herries, hero of Hugh Walpole's novel (see Watendlath for more on Walpole). Rosthwaite post office is a familiar landmark, usually full of walkers buying mars bars before setting off up the fells.

There is a bus to Rosthwaite from Keswick, roughly every ninety minutes. The valley is perhaps better as a base in early Spring or late Autumn, when the traffic has thinned and it is easier to get out of the valley to other parts of the Lake District. It really remains the essential province of the walker.

Watendlath   C ***

Watendlath is a small, attractive hamlet, standing beside a tarn, high above Borrowdale Valley. It's little more than a cluster of houses and farms, really. Despite its remoteness, and the fact that there is really little to do here unless you're a walker, Watendlath remains a popular spot in summer, mostly for its superb, picturesque setting.

A narrow, two-and-a-half mile long road winds 600 feet up the fellside to reach the hamlet, leaving the main Borrowdale road at a point north of the Lodore Hotel. On route, you encounter Ashness Bridge. This old packhorse bridge is one of the most photographed objects in the Lake District. Kodak must get sick of developing prints of it. It is a superb viewpoint, looking out over Derwent Water, with Cat Bells to the west and Skiddaw to the north. But at the height of the season, this road is a complete menace. Cars crammed along its length at all angles, trying to manouver round each other. If you value a low blood pressure, Watendlath is best reached by foot. Park in the small car park in the woods, just opposite Barrow Bay landing stage, and follow the road, or, better still, walk up from Rosthwaite village.

The hamlet sits in a fold on a wide, rolling mountain moor, with a tiny tarn alongside, complete with ducks. The packhorse bridge over the beck completes the picture. There's even a tea room, at the farm as you enter the village. An ideal spot to aim for, midway along a walk.

The packhorse route runs between Borrowdale and Wythburn, at the southern end of Thirlmere. Furness Abbey maintained a drove road along here, which extended to Rydal and Ambleside. One of Lakeland's most remote hamlets, it is only in recent years that it was connected to the national grid. The residents put up lights in a Christmas tree in the car park to celebrate. They took them all down again when they got their first electricity bill. Telephones didn't arrive until 1984.

The hamlet found literary fame in *The Herries Chronicles,* a series of novels written by Sir Hugh Walpole, tracing the life of a fictional family from the eighteenth century up to the 1930s. The books were all set in the Keswick area and at the time were mentioned in the same breath as Galsworthy's *Forsyth Saga.* The heroine of *Judith Paris,* the second novel in the series, was depicted living at Fold Head Farm, which stands at the southern end of the village. Now a bed and breakfast, the house bears a plaque which reads 'Judith Paris's Home'. Walpole's house, Brackenburn, where he wrote the novels, is situated on the western shore of Derwent Water (but is not open to the public).

Half way between Ashness Bridge and the village, there is the site of an ancient hill fort, just above Reecastle Crag.

Buttermere

FLAVOUR

Buttermere is the jewel of Borrowdale, the point most people make for, the one they all remember. It stands at the point where the valley opens out once again, after the climb over Honister Pass. The village stands between Buttermere lake and Crummock Water, at the junction of the B5289 and the Newlands Pass road. It is an attractive, pastoral spot, cut off from the outside world by the mountains. The road north-east, along Crummock Water to Lorton and Loweswater, is the only access for cars which doesn't involve a mountain pass (though Honister is pretty easy and Newlands Pass must be the kindest to engines in the LD).

FACTS

The village consists of a few farms, two well-known hotels and a number of stone-built houses strung along the main road in two distinct groups. It is an old farming community. The name Buttermere means 'the lake beside the pastures', referring to the flat, gentle farming land between the two lakes.

The Fish Hotel (originally the Fish Inn) was once the centre of a notable scandle, which has remained a popular subject for speculation right up to the present day. Towards the end of the eighteenth century, it was visited by Joseph Budworth, an eccentric writer and traveller, who was much taken by the innkeeper's daughter, Mary Robinson. He sang her praises in his guide to the area, *A Fortnight's Ramble in the Lakes*, which was published in 1792. As a result, Mary became a major tourist attraction as people flocked to the area, wanting to see this unspoilt Cumbrian beauty for themselves.

Mary Robinson remained immune to these attentions, until 1802, and the arrival in the area of the Honourable Alexander Augustus Hope, MP for Linlithgow. After feting the local gentry in Keswick and Grasmere, and running up huge debts, he came char fishing to Buttermere, but caught Mary instead. Everyone congratulated Mary on her sudden rise through the ranks of society and all went well until Coleridge, then correspondent for the London *Morning Post*, wrote up the marriage and, in the ensuing fuss, Hope was exposed as an imposter - the notorious swindler and bigamist, James Hatfield. Hatfield was arrested as soon as he and Mary returned from their honeymoon. He escaped over the mountains to Ravenglass, but was caught some months later, in Wales, and later tried and hung at Carlisle. Although the offence for which he was tried was not a capital one, the jury seem

Farmhouse at Buttermere

to have been swayed by the huge wave of public sympathy for Mary. Even Wordsworth got involved. He and Coleridge visited Hatfield in prison at Carlisle.

This classic tale of simple country folk despoiled by worldly blackguards from the big city promptly became a literary hit, even reaching the stage in Wordsworth's time. More recently, it has been the subject of a best-selling novel by a young local lad, Melvyn Bragg (*The Maid of Buttermere*, now available in paperback. Advt.). It might make an Andrew Lloyd Webber musical yet ...

BEST BUILDINGS

The tiny church is charming, situated just above the village, with a good aspect over the surrounding fields. It dates from the mid-nineteenth century.

WALKS

The area is familiar to walkers, with good access to Haystacks, High Stile, Dale Head and, for the more energetic, up onto Great Gable. It is also popular with less hardened ramblers; the four-mile circuit around Buttermere lake is one of Lakeland's easiest and most attractive walks. A good area to head for if you want to get outside and the weather is not so good. There's also a good walk to Scale Force, on Gale Fell, just west of the village.

STAYING

The are a couple of hotels, the **Fish Hotel** (Buttermere 253) and the **Bridge Hotel** (Buttermere 252), both quite small.

EATING

The **Bridge** does excellent bar meals, but can get very busy. Also a small cafe, just inside the village, opposite the Fish.

TRANSPORT

Getting here by public transport, you're thrown back on the Mountain Goat; regular service from Keswick, via Newlands Pass, but only between April and September (Keswick 73962). By car, Buttermere is only twenty minutes from Keswick if you come over the Newlands Pass, but considerably longer if you come via Borrowdale and Honister. There's a car park just inside Buttermere village, by Mill Beck, run by the National Park.

Tourist information   Moot Hall in Keswick.

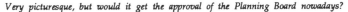

Very picturesque, but would it get the approval of the Planning Board nowadays?

Main Street, Cockermouth

Chapter 5

Cockermouth

Cockermouth   B ***

FLAVOUR

Cockermouth is proof that not all Lakeland gems lie inside the National Park boundary. For years, there has been talk of altering the line so that the town is included, and it would be no bad thing; it deserves a measure of recognition and protection.

Cockermouth is a fine, attractive market town. A wide, tree-lined main street and a number of Georgian town houses give it a (slightly spurious) air of prosperity. The town has a lot of pride in itself and there have been a number of building restored and repainted in recent years. In fact, Cockermouth is very up and coming. Just sufficiently outside the regular tourist orbit to make it attractive to locals wanting some peace and quiet. Popular with nuclear yuppies from BNFL.

For the visitor, it is the sort of place to save for a wet day. If the cloud drops, you're not missing any mountain scenery and you can spend an hour or two exploring the antiques market, the shops or wandering around Wordsworth's birthplace. In the winter, don't miss the Christmas lights. Not as vast and vulgar as Oxford Street, but very attractive.

The River Cocker cuts a broad swathe through the town; there are several places where you can explore its banks. Ignore the odd sign of a neglected building or an untidy car park, just enjoy the relative peace and quiet and convince yourself that you're discovering something the rest of Lakeland has yet to find.

FACTS

Cockermouth is one of Cumbria's most historic towns. Settlement of the area goes back to the Iron Age. In the second century A.D., the Romans built a fort, *Alavna*, at Papcastle, at the junction of the Roman roads to Maryport, Penrith and Carlisle. Cockermouth Castle was built around

87

1250 and the present town grew up about it. The basic street plan of the town has remained unchanged since medieval times, when the castle would have been the only stone built building Cockermouth. Turner stayed here in 1809, and his painting of the castle now hangs in the Turner Room at Petworth.

Cockermouth was granted a market charter in 1221, the second Cumbrian town to receive one. The following year, further permission was granted by Henry III to change market day from Saturday to Monday. The town quickly developed as an important market centre and had a reputation by 1671 as "ye best Market Towne in this part of ye county". It became second only to Kendal as an important centre for the wool trade. The town had its own Moot Hall, similar in appearance to the one at Keswick. It used to stand at the 'bend' of Market Place, but was demolished in 1829. A market bell, or 'butter bell', was rung to signal the start of the market. It still hangs in Market Place and was last used in 1910.

Always a town favoured by the gentry, a survey in 1665 found five families in Cockermouth who had their own coat of arms (by contrast, Carlisle at the time only had two, Penrith and Kendal one each).

Quarrying developed in the area, along with iron and lead mining. In 1861, the Cockermouth, Keswick and Penrith Railway Company was formed. The railway line remained open until 1966.

John Wordsworth was a land agent to the Lowther family and moved into the building now known as Wordsworth House in 1766. William and Dorothy were born here. The atomic theorist, John Dalton, was born in Eaglesfield, near Cockermouth, in 1766 and Robert Louis Stevenson stayed in the town in 1871. The statue in Main Street is Richard Southwell Bourke, the sixth Earl of Mayo. He was Viceroy and Govenor General of India when, in 1872, he was assassinated, stabbed in the Andamans.

Another notable resident was Fletcher Christian, the chief mutineer aboard the infamous *Bounty*. He was born locally in 1764 and was appointed chief mate under Captain Bligh in 1787.

BEST BUILDINGS

The finest house on Main Street is undoubtably **Wordsworth House,** built in 1746 and rather grand. Cumberland Motor Services bought it in 1937, with plans to demolish it and build a bus station, but there was a public outcry and the following year the house was bought by the National Trust.

A little farther along Main Street is the **United Reform Church,** the appearance of which comes as something of a shock; all Victorian Gothic, resembling the outside of a boy's public school. The centre of

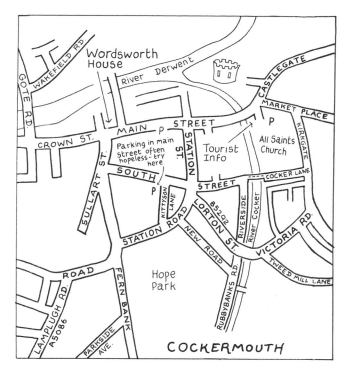

Map labels: Wordsworth House, River Derwent, WAKEFIELD RD, GOTE RD, CROWN ST., MAIN STREET, Parking in main street often hopeless – try here, SULLART ST., SOUTH STREET, STATION ST., Tourist Info, All Saints Church, MARKET PLACE, CASTLEGATE, KIRKGATE, COCKER LANE, KITTYSON LANE, LORTON ROAD, NEW ROAD, STATION ROAD, B5292, LORTON ST., RIVERSIDE, River Cocker, VICTORIA RD., TWEED MILL LANE, ROAD, FERN BANK, LAMPLUGH RD., A5086, PARKSIDE AVE., RUBBYBANKS RD., Hope Park, COCKERMOUTH

the street is dominated by a statue to the sixth **Earl of Mayo** (there is also a bust of Wordsworth, hiding rather coyly round the corner in Sullart Street, placed there in 1970 to commemorate his bicentenary). The **Old Courthouse** is interesting and dates from 1828. **The Globe Hotel** was built in 1750, on the site of an earlier, wooden inn.

Market Place is unusual in that the street goes through a right angle. You're immediately confronted by the **Ship Inn**, which has recently been restored and now looks very attractive. The buildings opposite were part of the old **Fletcher Old Hall**. The building dated from the seventeenth century but was substantially demolished in 1973. Mary Queen of Scots stayed here 1568, when fleeing from the English. Through the arched passage way is a small, cobbled courtyard with the curious name of Old Hall Went. The **market bell** still hands in Market Place, about fifteen feet up in the right hand corner of the building now occupied by a Chinese takeaway.

Turn up **Kirkgate** and, after a rough start, you find youself in Cockermouth's most attractive residential street. On the left is row of Georgian town houses set back from the road across a cobbled pavement. The houses opposite are smaller and were intended for less grand families. Just past the Third World shop, at the entrance to Cocker Lane, there is a path which takes you up to **All Saints Church**. This is very pretty sandstone church, built in the 1850s. The lane runs between the two halves of the churchyard and brings you down to the car park, behind Market Place.

Cockermouth Castle dates in part from the thirteenth century, but it was rebuilt in the fourteenth. Over the years it was passed through a number of hands, often given by the Crown to favoured individuals (Edward II, for example, gave it to Piers Gavestone in July 1309, but he gave it back again in August). It is now owned by Lord Egremont and still a private residence. Not generally open to the public, but sometimes tours are available during Cockermouth Festival. If you get in, look out for the vaulted underground chapel, called the Mirk Dirk.

THINGS TO DO

Plenty of shops, not really attempting to cater for the tourist, but perhaps the nicer for all that. There are a couple of bookshops in Main Street, both run by Winkworth's. One deals with new books, the other second hand. Small but interesting. Excellent Antique Market in the Old Courthouse, next to the bridge (Cockermouth 824346). Also try Cockermouth Antiques, in Station Street (Cockermouth 826746) and there is the New Art Gallery, in Castlegate. No cinema or theatre (the old Gaiety Theatre building is now a vet's surgery).

Wordsworth House, Main Street (Cockermouth 824805). Wordsworth's birthplace; his father was land agent for the Lowther family and William was the second of five children. Still much as it was in the poet's day, though the furniture is not Wordsworth's. Attractive garden and an excellent coffee kitchen. Owned and run by the National Trust.

Doll and Toy Museum, Market Place (Cockermouth 85259). Tucked down a narrow alley off Market Place, this is a large, fascinating collection of ethnic dolls from over 60 countries. The owners boast that it is the only collection of its kind in the country. There is also a tinplate model railway.

EVENTS

Cockermouth Show - small local show, held at the beginning of August. Details from the tourist information centre.

WALKS

No fells to launch yourself up, but some attractive field walks along the banks of the Cocker; either turn off Gote Road, or head south over the old railway embankment.

STAYING

Try the **Ship Inn**, in Market Place (Cockermouth 823091). There are also a few smaller B&Bs, tucked away in the side streets. Cockermouth makes a peaceful, relaxing base from which to explore the Lakes. The travelling time to get into the National Park makes it a bit frantic to include the southern lakes in a day, but you've a nice, friendly place to retreat to.

EATING

Good for coffees and snacks; try the attractive **Courtyard Coffee House**, Headford Court (Cockermouth 823971). The cafe in Wordsworth House is good, but only open to those who go through the house. A good restaurant is the **Old Court House**, beside the bridge in Main Street (Cockermouth 823871) and there is a new vegetarian restaurant, **Quince and Medlar**, at the bottom of Castlegate (Cockermouth 823579). Perhaps the mosat attractive place for light snacks is **Over the Top** in Kirkgate (Cockermouth 827016).

TRANSPORT

On the main bus route from Whitehaven to Keswick, with connections south, into the lakes, out to Penrith and up to Carlisle. (Cumberland Bus Company, Whitehaven 3781). The trip to Keswick takes forty minutes, with a bus every hour. Cockermouth to the M6 (junction 40) is about 30 miles, but quite quick along the A66. Parking in town is straightforward, with on-street parking (restricted) and good, central car parks in South Street and Market Place.

Tourist information in the Riverside Car Park, just off Market Street (Cockermouth 822634).

Market day Monday, early closing Thursday.

Isel   ℂ **

Inspect a large scale Ordnance Survey map of the Cockermouth area and you might, if you use a magnifying glass, spot a minute hamlet called Isel (it's eight inches to the north east on the 1:25000 series). Drive round looking for it, and it is even harder to find; there's no centralised settlement, just a mill and a couple of cottages next to **Isel Hall**, the large mansion overlooking the River Derwent. This is a private home, and consists of a largely sixteenth century mansion built onto a pele tower. Very well sited but not itself very beautiful.

The reason for seeking out Isel is to find the church. This stands half-a-mile south of the hall, just off the road, beside a patch woodland on the banks of the Derwent. **St Michael's** is a small and very ancient building, situated at what may have been a crossing point on the river. The river is still very wide and peaceful here and at that time the whole area would have been thick forest (Derwent means 'the river of oaks'). Much of the present church is Norman, though there was some restoration in the late nineteenth century. The chancel arch inside is much as it was when it was constructed in 1130, and the tiny slit windows in the north wall date from the same period. When the church was restored, many of the original roofing timbers were retained.

Next to the chancel window is a fragment of carved stone, known as the Triskele Stone. This is part of an early Christian cross - though at one time there was some debate that it might even be fourth or fifth century.

Isel used to be spelt 'Isell' - the final 'l' was dropped early this century. The parish still refers to itself in the old way. You can park next to the church and there is a pleasant footpath on the far side of the river.

Bassenthwaite   ℂ *

Bassenthwaite village is easily missed as it is not on the lake - it's about a mile-and-a-half from the northern shores. It has a village green, two churches, a pub and a charming, chattering river - Chapel Beck. The approach to this quiet farming village from the A591 is down a winding, hedge-lined lane. There are one or two pleasant cottages, but nothing of stunning architectural significance in the main village. **The Sun Inn** (Bassenthwaite Lake 439) is a nice old pub and does some of the best bar meals in the Lakes (excellent lasagne, if you've grown tired of Cumber-

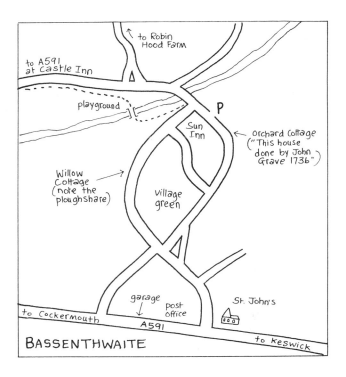

to Robin
Hood Farm

to A591
at Castle Inn

playground

Sun
Inn

P

orchard Cottage
("This house
done by John
Grave 1736")

Willow
Cottage
(note the
ploughshare)

village
green

garage

post
office

St. John's

to Cockermouth

A591

BASSENTHWAITE

to Keswick

land sausage). Orchard Cottage, just opposite, bears a sign over the door which reads "This house done by John Grave 1736".

St John's Church, beside the A591, is a Victorian affair, described by Pevsner as "pretentious' and no one seems to have a good word for its endearingly fussy spire. **St Bega's Church**, however, is an altogether different affair. This stands two miles south, alone, in the fields beside Bassenthwaite Lake. It's charming, tiny and probably the most romantically situated church in Cumbria. To reach it, you have to follow a footpath across the fields (park at Dodd Wood and follow the public right of way behind Mirehouse - see below).

The building is Norman, but its small, circular churchyard and position next to a running stream suggest that it may have had much pagan origins. St Bega was an Irish noblewoman who founded the seventh century Benedictine nunnery at what is now St Bees. Alfred Lord Tennyson used the setting of the church in his epic Arthurian poem, *Morte d'Arthur*; St Bega's is the "chapel in the fields" where the dying King Arthur was carried by Sir Bedivere before he was borne away across the "great water". In earlier times, worshippers came here by boat, though now they have to walk across the fields. There is a stone cross just outside the churchyard which is occasionally used for open air services.

Within sight of the church, set among the trees, is **Mirehouse**, a Georgian manor house. This is one of the most attractive houses in Cumbria, with a unique atmosphere. The original, central part of the house was built at a hunting lodge in 1666, by the 8th Earl of Derby. In 1802, it was left to John Spedding, of Armathwaite Hall. Spedding was a contemporary of Wordsworth (they were in the same class at Hawkshead Grammar School) and his youngest son, James, was a close friend of Tennyson and Thomas Carlyle. Tennyson stayed here whilst writing *Morte d'Arthur*. These connections have left valuable family records and Mirehouse has remained in the Spedding family. It is open to the public, though on a deliberately low key basis, and is a delightful, charming place to visit. (For opening times, telephone Keswick 72287.)

Across the road from Mirehouse is the car park for Dodd Wood and the **Old Sawmill Cafe**. The cafe is in the original mill building, built around 1880. Inside are a number of forestry tools and photographs on display. Park here to explore the house and St Bega's. There are also some good forest walks - the Dodd is a good viewpoint, a short walk from the car park. Or you can follow a path through the woods along the east side of the A591 to the Ravenstone Hotel, cross the main road and continue through the fields to St Bega's, coming back via Mirehouse.

Lorton   ℂ *

The Vale of Lorton is arguably the prettiest of the Lakeland valleys. Wordsworth used to rave about it. It runs from Cockermouth, south to include Crummock Water and Buttermere, ending where it meets the Honister Pass.

The village of Lorton is signposted as two parts - High Lorton and Low Lorton, though there is scarcely a quarter of a mile between them. **High Lorton** is at the western end of Newlands Pass and is the larger of the two. The houses are strung along the main road for perhaps half a mile. As you pass through from the north, the most puzzling feature is the high wall on your right. This encompassses **Lorton Park** and the rather fine house associated with it stands at the north of the village. To the side of the house, just visible from the road, is a tiny castellated tower.

There's a craft centre and cafe in the village, **White Ash Barn** (Lorton 236).

Farther south, just before the post office and general store, is an old terrace, a row of workers' cottages dating from the period when there was a mill and a thriving flax industry in the village.

Continue down the main road, turn right at the crossroads and you follow a narrow lane to **St Cuthbert's Church**, which stands roughly between High and Low Lorton. There has been a church on this site for at least eight hundred years, though the present version dates from 1809. The inside is rather grandios and the highly coloured stained glass window and arch give it a very theatrical appearance. St Cuthbert died in 687 A.D. and his body was carried off by monks, fleeing the Danes. Their reputed resting places have caused a number of St Cuthbert's churches to spring up all over Northern England.

Low Lorton lies west of the church (there is a public footpath across the field to the village). **Lorton Hall** is one of the few pele towers to have strayed in amongst the central fells of Lakeland. It is a fifteenth century pele tower with seventeenth and nineteenth century additions. There was an earlier Hall on this site, going back to perhaps the early nineth century. Also in the village is the local pub, the Wheatsheaf Inn.

Tourist information is available at the post office and store in High Lorton.

Loweswater   ℂ *

Not really a village, Loweswater is more of a straggle of houses between Loweswater Lake and Crummockwater. It is an excellent spot for lake walks. The lake takes its name from the woodland around its shores (it means 'leafy lake'). Holme Wood, on the south-west shore, is a very pleasant walk. There is a nice little church, **St Batholomew's**, built by the villagers in 1827. Good bar meals at the **Kirkstile Inn** (Lorton 219). First class 'country house' accomodation at the **Scale Hill Hotel** (Lorton 232) but it is wise to book in advance, as it has become very popular with those in the know.

Whitehaven Harbour

Chapter 6

Whitehaven

Whitehaven **

FLAVOUR

Whitehaven is for those who are absolutely determined to get off the beaten track, well away from the crowds of Lakeland. To get there from Keswick, you have twenty eight miles of boring main road, giving you plenty of time to reflect upon all those wonderful fells that you're leaving behind. As you hit the outskirts of town, and begin to encounter dreary housing estates and signs of industrialisation, your resolve weakens further. But persist; practically alone among the West Cumbrian towns, Whitehaven is fighting hard to shed the legacy of industrial decline. There is nice town in there, struggling to get out.

Go to the docks and it's hard to believe that this port once rivalled Liverpool. There's a wild, neglected, windswept air. Look back at the houses, and the town seems to have turned its back on the harbour, preferring to look inward. But stay here long enough and you'll see signs of activity. There are still Things Happening in Whitehaven. There's a thriving chemical industry on the outskirts, and a lot of much-needed money has been pumped into the town by BNFL, simply to make it an attractive place to live. The place has a lot of potential. Another good indicator is the presence of some of the major retail stores in the town - usually a sign of a place with a future.

The central part of town is set out in the form of a grid. The one way system runs around the outside, while in the centre itself the streets are being increasingly pedestrianised, which is a boon. The town centre is, in the main, filled with pleasant, Georgian houses, some of which bear obvious signs of their maritime and trading heritage; look out for pulleys and loading doors, above the shops and main entrances. Some streets are very attractive, others have odd buildings here and there which still show signs of neglect. Areas like Queen Street are being tidied up - the little courtyard opposite The Good Food Shop is very attractive, only lacking a couple of gas lamps to complete the scene.

There are some fascinating rooflines, interesting shop fronts and in general signs that people are working hard to attract visitors to the area. But the effect is still a bit piecemeal. There's a long way to go yet and although there is much that is nice about Whitehaven, it helps to have a sense of history to colour your vision.

FACTS

This area was once all sand dunes - a fact commemorated by names such as Sandhills Lane. The harbour was known to the Norse - the name comes from *hvit hafn* or the 'white haven' (a reference to the white stone headland to the south). At one time it must have been a tiny fishing village. In 1633 it was a hamlet of nine houses.

During the seventeenth century, the Lowthers owned large estates along the west coast. The presence of coal on their Whitehaven estate provided the impetous for the development of the town as a port. In 1634, Christopher Lowther built a pier, to facilitate the arrival of shipping from Dublin. His son, Sir John Lowther, threw himself into developing the town; by 1700 Whitehaven was a burgeoning port with a population over 2,000. Liverpool at this time had a merchant fleet of eighty-four ships, whereas Whitehaven had seventy-seven. Sir John bought ship building to the town and it remained an important industry for the next two hundred years; the last ship constructed at Whitehaven was the *Englehorn*, a four mast baroque, launched in 1889 - the last of an estimated 684 vessels built at the port.

It was during the lifetime of his son, Sir James, that Whitehaven was developed along the grid pattern still present today. It remains the earliest post-medieval planned town in England. Although elegant in the eighteenth century, it later led to dreadful overcrowding and slums as the original spacious and elegant gardens were built over and the streets filled in to provide accomodation for workers. In the 1930s and 40s so much housing was declared unsafe or unfit for habitation, that a large new council estate was built just outside town, on the hill to the south west - an area many modern developers must covet for the tremendous views of the town and harbour.

During the American War of Independence, in 1778, Captain John Paul Jones attempted to set fire to the entire merchant fleet at Whitehaven. Born in Kirkcudbrightshire in 1747, at the age of twelve he was apprenticed to a merchant seaman at Whitehaven. After a varying career, at the outbreak of the war he joined the newly-formed Congressional Navy and was eventually dispatched on a privateering mission around the British coast to do as much damage to the enemy as possible. After once false start at Whitehaven, he and some of his men rowed in during the early hours of the morning of 23 April. After spiking the guns

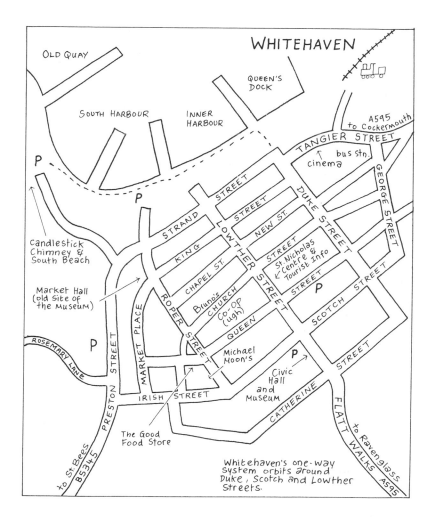

WHITEHAVEN

OLD QUAY

QUEEN'S DOCK

SOUTH HARBOUR

INNER HARBOUR

A595 to Cockermouth

TANGIER STREET

bus stn.

cinema

P

STRAND STREET

LOWTHER STREET

NEW ST.

DUKE STREET

GEORGE STREET

Candlestick Chimney & South Beach

KING STREET

CHAPEL ST.

Bruno's

CHURCH STREET

STREET

St. Nicholas Centre & Tourist Info

STREET

SCOTCH STREET

STREET

P

Market Hall (old Site of the Museum)

ROPER STREET

Co-op (ugh)

QUEEN STREET

P

P

ROSEMARY LANE

PRESTON STREET

MARKET PLACE

Michael Moon's

Civic Hall and Museum

P

CATHERINE STREET

FLATT WALKS

to Ravenglass A595

IRISH STREET

The Good Food Store

to St. Bees B5345

Whitehaven's one-way system orbits around Duke, Scotch and Lowther Streets.

of the harbour battery, they succeeded in setting fire to one ship before the alarm was given and they were forced to retreat. The attack was unsuccessful, though Jones went on to achieve the status as a sort of maritime bogeyman.

Whitehaven was developed on the back of the local coalfield. In the eighteenth century, a pit was sunk which extended three-quarters of a mile under the seabed. In 1900, the collieries employed over 2,181 men and extracted 536,493 tons of coal. Metal and chemical industries grew up associated with the coal mining, helping to take some of the brunt as pits began to close around the 1920s and 30s. There is still a thriving chemical plant, the Marchon Works, now owned by Albright and Wilson. Farther down the coast, the presence of Sellafield has led to massive BNFL investment in the area and an influx of new residents.

BEST BUILDINGS

Some interesting and attractive old buildings in the area of the docks. The pier known as **Old Quay** was built around 1687 and still has its short, stubby lighthouse, dating from 1730. Just inland is the South Beach Recreational area; the **Candlestick Chimney** there is part of the old Wellington coal pit surface building. Built around 1840, the design was allegedly based on a candlestick in Whitehaven Castle. The **Castle** itself stands in Lowther Street; built in 1769 as Flatt Hall, the home of Sir John Lowther, it was sold in 1924 to become the Whitehaven and West Cumberland Hospital (now superceded by the large, modern hospital on the outskirts of town). Back in the docks area, look out for the large green and black building at the head of Duke Street, on the corner of Tangier Street. The colour scheme is a bit lurid, but there's some amazing stucco work along the top of the building.

Shame about the **Baths House**, just opposite. Now in a state of considerable neglect, it must have been quite attractive at one time. On a happier note, there are some fine Georgian town houses in **Scotch Street**. **St James Church**, Queen Street, has one of the finest Georgian interiors in England. The original **St Nicholas Church**, in Lowther Street, dated from 1693, but all that remains is the present doorway. Not much left of the second version, either, which was largely burnt down in 1971. The tower survived and is now a sort of church/community centre/cafe. Superb modern engraved glass screen. The tourist information centre sits rather uncomfortably in the entrance porch. The churchyard is laid out like a garden, the tombstones set flat. Mildred Warner Gale, the grandmother of George Washington, was buried here. This area remains very pleasant and the ruins of the church building have been nicely converted into a small square.

At the time of writing, a lot of work is being done on the **Town Hall**, in Duke Street, which should be attractive when finished. One can only hope that it isn't too long before the **Market Hall** is restored and the museum put back where it belongs.

Despite the work being done to preserve the older buildings, there are still some which are very run down. Worse still are the 1960's style buildings which have been dropped with a complete lack of sympathy into the midst of the older streets. The Co-Op block in Roper Street is a particularly revolting example, totally out of character with its surroundings. Meanwhile, the Presto supermarket is actually grafted onto the back of the old Catholic church. Must be the most ecclesiastical retail establishment in Cumbria.

The Civic Hall, in Lowther Street, is neat, modern, functional and nothing to write home about. The new police building, in Scotch Street, has been described as "the ugliest nick in Britain". No self-respecting architecture buff would dare commit a crime in Whitehaven for fear that he would end up in it. And who's bright idea was it to locate a Leicester Square-type 'Tardis toilet' in Market Place?

THINGS TO DO

Plenty of shops and a welcome relief from the gifte-type shops seen elsewhere in the Lakes. You can go a whole day without seeing a Lakeland sheepskin or a Genuine Scottish woollen. A fair number of representatives of the larger retail chains have made it to Whitehaven (presumably on missionary work) but don't let that put you off.

Whitehaven Museum, Lowther Street (Whitehaven 3111, extension 307). Now located in the Civic Hall; used to be in the Market Hall, a much nicer building, but the tower was beginning to part company with the roof ... The move means that the museum has lost much of its charm and now has the air of a temporary travelling exhibition. Still some good exhibits - fine model ships; an engagingly revolting account of a preserved, mummified, thirteenth century nobleman, found at St Bees; and a splendid, bird's eye view of the town, painted in 1736 by Metthias Read. Open all year round and admission free.

Michael Moon's, Roper Street (Whitehaven 62936). Wonderful second-hand bookshop. Probably the best - certainly the most entertaining - in Cumbria. A sort of swashbuckling, second-hand book seller, Mr Moon not only buys and sells old books, but publishes them as well, reprinting charming works of local interest which have been long out of print. His latest enterprise is a small exhibition gallery at the back of the shop, which will feature displays ranging from paintings to old bookmarks. Good place to head for, whatever the weather (visitors have been known to come to look round Whitehaven and end up spending all day at Moon's).

Evenings: There used to be two cinemas and a theatre in the town centre, but now, alas, nearly all gone. Only half a cinema left, **The Gaiety** (Whitehaven 3012), in Tangier Street (half a cinema, dear reader, because screen two is now a bingo hall). Good theatre just outside town, the **Rosehill Theatre** (Whitehaven 2422) at Moresby. A positive breath of culture in an area where you otherwise face a long trek to see a play or hear a concert. There's even a restaurant on site.

WALKS

Not much from within the town centre. Good, bracing cliff walks south of town, onto St Bees Head.

STAYING

Good as a base for the western fells and lakes, hopeless for the central Lakes - it's just that bit too far out. Try the **Waverley Hotel** (Whitehaven 4337) or the **Chase Hotel** (Whitehaven 3656).

EATING

There is a very good Italian restaurant and wine bar, **Bruno's**, in Church Street (Whitehaven 65270). For snacks, try **The Good Food Store**, Queen Street (Whitehaven 66628). Reasonable bar meals at **Victor's**, Market Place (Whitehaven 65464). The **Civic Hall** does good lunches. Good coffees in the **St Nicholas Centre**.

TRANSPORT

Bus links to Cockermouth, Workington and Barow (Barrow? How did that creep in?), also connections to Keswick (bus station in Tangier Street, Whitehaven 3781). Also rail - yes, rail, it's almost like being back in civilisation, isn't it? - telephone Whitehaven 2414. The railway is part of the coast line, between Barrow and Carlisle, so be warned; it could take ages to get anywhere. By car, it is about half-an-hour to Keswick - roughly the same to Ravenglass. The one-way system round Duke, Scotch, Lowther and Tangier Streets can be bewildering at first. Take the first opportunity to dive into a car park. Restricted parking on the streets (and it gets so crowded its hardly worth it, unless you're a streetwise native). Good car park by the harbour, just off Strand Street. If it's nice weather and you don't mind a short walk, try the one on South Beach. Also a multi-storey car park in Preston Street.

Tourist information St Nicholas Centre, Lowther Street (Whitehaven 5678). Can't be many churches in the country which harbour a tourist information centre.

Market day Thursday and Saturday, early closing Wednesday.

Ravenglass

FLAVOUR

Isolated on the coast, at the extreme western edge of the LD National Park, Ravenglass is notable as the home of La'al Ratty railway and as somewhere to aim for as an excuse to go over the Wrynose and Hardknott Pass. It's a bit of a 'one-horse' village these days; a quiet main street, a few boats, some nice sand dunes - nothing to get terribly excited about. You get the feeling the place has been left outside too long, and now it's gently rusting away.

At the end of the short main street are a pair of flood gates. Pass through and you're on the beach, looking across the small, silted-up harbour to Eskmeal Dunes. This is the site of a Gullery and Nature Reserve (and not to be confused with the Gunnery and Firing Range a little farther down the coast, a sort of unnatural reserve for the MOD).

FACTS

Before it silted up, Ravenglass was an important port; in Roman times it was the second largest port in Britain, the only natural harbour on the west coast between the Dee and the Solway. It was still active as a port, with sailings through to Liverpool, right up until the end of the eight-

Looking across the estuary to Ravenglass

eenth century. The harbour is still used, mainly by small yachts and the occassional windsurfer.

The Romans built an important fort here, *Glannaventa*, but unfortunately little now remains. The final remenants were destroyed by the Victorians when they brought the main railway line through, towards the end of the last century.

The Ravenglass and Eskdale Railway (or 'La'al Ratty' as it is known to the locals) arrived in 1875. Originally a 3' wide guage line (it's now fifteen inches), it was built to transport haematite from the iron mines at Boot to the main Furness line. It has had a chequered history, suffering from the closure of the mines in 1882, when it was left to be a tourist attraction (it promoted itself as "the route to the English Alps"). In its prime, it was the area's major employer (that accolade has now gone to BNFL). It suffered several changes of use and ownership, until 1960, when the Ravenglass and Eskdale Preservation Society bought the line at public auction for £12,000. The following year, the Ravenglass and Eskdale Railway Company Limited was formed and since then there has been large-scale rebuilding of the line. Today it is the valley's major tourist attraction.

BEST BUILDINGS

Not a lot to see on the main street of Ravenglass itself. The Pennington Arms Hotel is quite impressive, otherwise you have to delve off into the undergrowth in search of **Walls Castle**. This was the bath house to the ancient Roman fort. It stands, screened by trees, a little way outside the village, where it was presumably hidden from the attentions of the Victorian workmen. It has the highest standing walls of any Roman ruin in the North of England, over twelve feet high in places. You can still see they layout of the rooms, the position of the windows.

THINGS TO DO

The obvious thing, for a start, is a ride on **La'al Ratty**. Seven miles of track winding through lovely countryside along the northern flanks of Muncaster Fell. Most of the engines are steam driven, lovingly cared for and very attractive. The line is actually scheduled in British Rail's timetables, bringing commutors down the valley to the mainline train, so it runs all year round, though only two or three per weekday in winter. (Telephone Ravenglass 226.)

On the station is the small **Ravenglass Railway Museum** (Ravenglass 226). Gives the history of the trains and the valley. Worth a look. One of the stopping points on the line is **Muncaster Mill** (Ravenglass 232). An old cornmill, dating back to the 1700s, it was restored in the

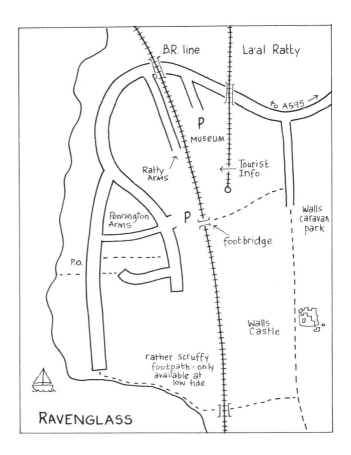

RAVENGLASS

1970s and is now open to the public. The manager, Peter Ellis, runs it as a working exhibition, even milling his own flour during quiet periods. Lovely, idyllic setting.

Slightly farther afield is **Muncaster Castle** (Ravenglass 614), the family seat of the Penningtons. Originally a pele tower, it had a fine mansion built on and now stands in magnificent grounds on a natural shelf on the southern side of Muncaster view. Tremendous views from the terrace. The house itself is interesting and the gardens house a bird garden and the British Owl Breeding and Release Scheme.

Ravenglass Gullery and Nature Reserve has the largest breeding colony of black headed gulls in Europe, along with a variety of other waders and gulls. Restricted access, so you have to get a permit from the County Land Agent, Carlisle (Carlisle 23456).

WALKS

Good walks south of the village, past Walls Castle and towards Muncaster Castle; there's a public right of way through the grounds, which is very attractive. Best walk in the area is undoubtably along the summit of Muncaster Fell. Brilliant views out to the Isle of Man. Leave the car at Dalegarth Station, catch the railway to Ravenglass and walk back.

STAYING

Ravenglass is a good base if you want lovely countryside and want to be well out of the crowds in Central Lakeland. Try the **Pennington Arms Hotel** (Ravenglass 222), on the main street or **St Michael's Country Guest House** (Ravenglass 362), just outside the village. A couple of B&Bs in the village, otherwise look farther afield; **Foldgate Farm** (Bootle 660), just down the coast at Bootle, is very good. Similarly, the **Bower House Inn** (Eskdale 244), back towards Eskdale Green is recommended.

EATING

Bower House Inn does wonderful pub meals. **The Ratty Arms** (Ravenglass 676) is good pub in the village itself.

TRANSPORT

Well, you've got the Ratty. Good for getting up and down the valley in summer, and a good way to link up a walk. Getting to Ravenglass itself, there is British Rail (unfortunately, it is an unmanned station, so for timetable enquiries ring Barrow-in-Furness 20805). By car, it is a long trip from the Central Lakes over the two steepest passes; allow an hour from Ambleside - after all, you don't want to take those 1 in 3 gradients and hairpin bends too quickly. Good parking in Ravenglass, either at the station or the National Park one nearby.

Tourist information Next door to the Ravenglass and Eskdale ticket office, telephone Ravenglass 278.

Boot

An attractive little hamlet, set in stunning countryside amidst the fells and fields of Eskdale. Not a lot to it; a few picturesque cottages, a craft gallery, a farm, an inn and a corn mill. But it is neat and attractively kept. You couldn't spend a great deal of time here, but it is nice to pass through.

Boot grew up with the discovery of iron ore in the fellside to the north. The Whitehaven Iron Mines Company operated Nab Gill mine and built the Ratty railway line to service it. The company folded in 1882, but mining and quarrying continued in the area until well into the twentieth century. The present Dalegarth Terminus - now the head of the line - was built beside the road in 1926.

The **Corn Mill**, at the top of the narrow road which runs through the village, has been restored and is now run by Cumbria County Council (details available on Kendal 21000). No longer a working mill, but some interesting machinery inside. Another interesting old building is the parish church of Eskdale, **St Catherine's**. It occupies a beautiful spot by the River Esk, a few hundred yards down the lane opposite the Brook House Hotel. A tiny building, with some interesting tombstones in the churchyard (look out for one belonging to Tommy Dobson, master of Eskdale Hunt; at one time his fame rivalled that of John Peel, the other great huntsman, from Caldbeck).

Another attraction lies a couple of miles east of the village, at the summit of Hardknott Pass. This is the ruin of the Roman fort of *Mediobogdum*, sometimes referred to in guide books as Hardknott Castle. The massively thick walls still stand to a height of three or four feet and it is easy to follow the layout of what was once an auxilary fort occupied by the Fourth Cohort of Dalmations. A tremendous position, built on a dramatic spur of mountainside to stand guard over the Roman road to Ravenglass. Spectacular views down the valley on a clear day.

Eskdale is a brilliant area for walks: try the route to Eel Tarn, just above the village. A good afternoon ramble with superb views across to the Scafell range. Or follow the track past St Catherine's and follow the riverside path upstream to Doctor Bridge; return along the opposite bank, emerging by the St George IV pub at Eskdale Green.

Gosforth

Travelling from the south, you approach Gosforth along one of the most scenic stretches of main road in Cumbria. It's lined with hedges, and flanked by fields, just like being back in real countryside.

Gosforth lies just off the A595 and is probably one of Lakeland's least visited large villages. It consists of a short main street, a couple of side streets and one or two uninteresting - though largely unobtrusive - modern bungalow estates. The main street is not architecturally beautiful, but the houses are plain, neat and straightforward. It is a quiet, slightly windswept village. There have been one or two attempts to cater for visitors. There a National Park information caravan in the car park. The **Arts and Crafts Centre** (Gosforth 258) has a cafe, and the **Gosforth Pottery** (Gosforth 296) is rather nice.

Gosforth Cross and St Mary's Church

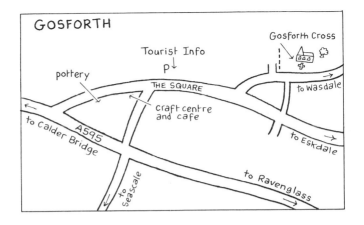

The star of Gosforth is the eleventh century cross in St Mary's Churchyard. This tall, slender cross, covered in intricate carvings, is one of the finest in Britain, yet stands only yards from the main road. Like Walls Castle, you feel it needs to be preserved in a glass case before it is too late.

St Mary's itself is large and plain from the outside but rather splendid inside. It has a lovely wooden ceiling and some nice stained glass. Look out for the woven cushions along the pine pews. The present church dates from 1789, but there was a building on this site in the early twelfth century. In the north-east corner of the knave are a pair of Norse hogback tombstones, uncovered when the church underwent its obligatory Victorian 'improvement' in 1896. The carvings on these stones are as fine as any you'll find in Cumbria. Alongside them is a model of Gosforth Cross, made by local school children in 1953.

Don't leave the church without looking for the **Chinese Bell**. It stands on a window sill in the west wall. It is covered in Chinese inscription and was captured at Anunghoy Fort, on the Canton River, in 1841, by Sir Humphrey le Fleming Senhouse. When his widow presented it to the church, the local blacksmith added a clapper (Chinese bells don't have them) and it was hung in a specially built arch. Unfortunately, it cracked the first time it was rung, so they took it down again and brought it inside. The stone cannon balls on either side of the bell came from the Dardanelles fort during the Crimea War.

Finally, in the churchyard you will find a cork tree, planted by James Lowther Senhouse, rector of Gosforth, in 1833. It is reputed to be the northern-most cork tree growing in England.

Tourist information National Park information caravan in the car park, telephone Gosforth 285.

Penrith Cornmarket

Chapter 7

Penrith

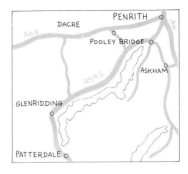

Penrith **

FLAVOUR

Penrith is a bustling market town with a no-nonsense air about it, as if it can't be bothered with all that fells and lakes stuff a few miles to the west. Once you immerse yourself in the town centre, it is hard to believe that you're less than five miles from Ullswater. Penrith seems to exist in a sort of limbo between the Lakes and the Borders, not ready to identify with either of them.

When you see the new housing estates, the industrial areas and the lorries thundering past, it is hard to remember that Penrith is little larger than Kendal in terms of strict geographical size. It has retained the feel of a market town and is a popular and attractive shopping centre; not as large and soulless as Carlisle and with fewer crowds and traffic problems than Kendal.

Penrith has always been known as the 'old red town', because of the rust coloured sandstone which features so prominantly in the construction of many of its buildings. It is a very historical town, with many attractive features. Staying here can be a bit like being on an island, within view of the mainland, but in reality it has a lot more to offer. There are the Pennines to the east, Carlisle and the Borders to the north and right on Penrith's doorstep, the lush countryside of the Eden Valley.

FACTS

The spot where Penrith stands was once woodland, part of the great Forest of Inglewood. Settlements may have grown up during the Bronze Age, but little evidence has been found of them. The first real event in Penrith's history came when the Romans established a fort just north of here, *Voreda*, one of a line along the road between York and

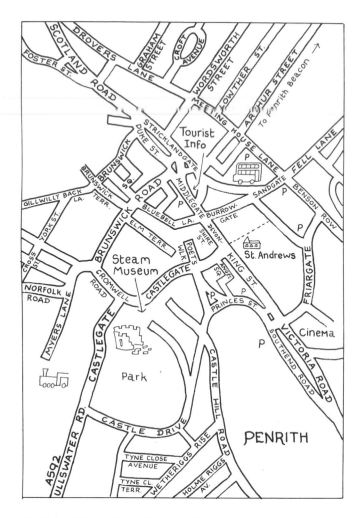

PENRITH

Carlisle. They chose this site for its proximity to a major crossing point on the River Eamont. The name Penrith derives from Old English for 'the chief ford'.

Penrith suffered from existing in the no-man's land between England and Scotland and was the subject of numerous border skirmishes, even after Edward I seized the area for England in 1295. A castle was built here by William Strickland (later to become Bishop of Carlisle) in 1397. It grew from a pele tower to a large, walled fortification but seems to have been in active use for only a couple of centuries and by the sixteenth century had become a rich source of building material for the locals.

In 1223, Henry III granted the town the right to hold a market and an annual fair. Penrith developed as a thriving market town. A clock tower now stands on the site of the original market cross, in Market Place. The cross was demolished - along with Penrith's Moot Hall - in the early years of the nineteenth century.

Plague hit Penrith at the end of the sixteenth century, killing 2,260 people. As a safeguard against infection from the surrounding countryfolk, the inhabitants mounted a large block of stone at the southern entrance to the town, known as the Plague Stone. A hollow centre contained a disinfectant (possibly vinegar) and was used to wash coins when transactions occured.

Penrith has had its share of notable visitors. Charles, the Young Pretender, stayed at the George Hotel, during the '45 Rebellion. John MacAdam (famous for his major contribution to road safety) lived at Cockell House, in Drovers Lane. Ta, Mac. Anthony Trollope stayed for a time at Carleton Hill. But the most famous resident was William Wordsworth, who lived here with his sister Dorothy, following the death of their parents. He and Dorothy attended Anne Birkett's dame school, overlooking St Andrew's church. One of their school chums was Mary Hutchinson, William's future wife.

Devonshire Street - do not expect parking here to be this easy today.

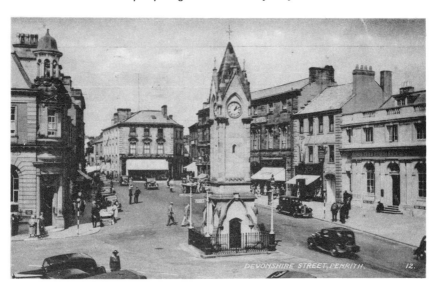

BEST BUILDINGS

There is a very fine church, **St Andrew's**, which stands in a churchyard, surrounded by attractive Georgian houses. This stately, red sandstone building dates from the 1720s, but stands on the site of an earlier church, built in the twelfth century. Only the west tower remains of the original building. There was probably a chapel on this site in Saxon times. There are a couple of fascinating curiousities in the churchyard: The **Giant's Grave** is a combination of two eleventh century crosses and four hogback tombstones. Legend has it that this is the grave of Owen Caesarius, the tenth century King of Cumbria, but this is somewhat unlikely. At the northern entrance to the churchyard is another Anglian cross, known locally as the **Giant's Thumb**.

The two oldest streets in Penrith are **Burrowgate** and **Sandgate**; documentary mention of them goes back to the late thirteenth century. Friargate commemorates the existance in Penrith of an Augustinian friary, from 1291 until its dissolution in 1539. Nothing now remains of the building. The narrow passage between Devonshire Street and King Street - where traffic lights control the flow as only one line of cars can get through at a time - may have once been a cunning piece of town planning, designed to slow down marauding Scots from the north.

The **Castle** is rather a sad ruin, looking at first glance like a partly-demolished factory. The grounds are now a park, so its possible to wander around in the empty shell, though there is not much left. Some of the walls and rooms are labelled, so you can get an idea of the layout of the place.

Robinson's School, in Middlegate, dates from 1670 and now houses the tourist information centre. On the hill overlooking town, is **Penrith Beacon**, a monument to the 1745 rebellion and at one time this was the site for one of the great bonfires which established a line of communication along the valley, to warn of invasion from the north.

There are some good ancient buildings in the countryside around Penrith: the site of the Roman fort is five miles north of the town, just off the A6, overlooking the river Petterill. Not much to see now. A mile or so east of Penrith, just off the A66, is **Brougham Castle**, a magnificent thirteenth century ruin which stands on the site of the Roman fort of *Brocavum*.

Finally, at nearby Eamont Bridge are a pair of fascinating Neolithic monuments. **Mayburgh Henge** is a very impressive circular mound, a banked ring, up to fifteen feet high in places. In the centre is a single nine feet high standing stone. This solitary monolith is all that remains of two concentric circles of stones which once stood here. The site dates back to 2000B.C., and has a very sombre, brooding air about it.

King Arthur's Round Table stands just by the junction of the B5320 and the A6 and is a large mound, though the stones have now long

The Wine Shop, Penrith (but you probably guessed that already). Why is the man queueing to be served still wearing his pyjamas?

since disappeared. There was a burial mound at the centre of the monument. Thought to be slightly newer than Mayburgh (around 1800 B.C.) and absolutely nothing to do with King Arthur.

THINGS TO DO

Penrith is popular with locals for shopping, drawing people in from a large area, especially on market day.There are a number of smaller, family-run shops, in addition to representatives of the large multiples. Poet's Walk is a pleasant, small shopping arcade and there is an attractive new pedestrianised shopping area, Angel Square, just off Market Square. The Bluebell Bookshop, in Anglel Square, boasts that it is the largest in Cumbria. It is certainly one of the most interesting for *new* books - and it has a tearoom upstairs.

Penrith Steam Museum (Penrith 62154), Castlegate. Large museum catering for steam buffs of all ages. Extensive display of steam engines, engineering and agricultural machinery. The machines are often in steam, but ring to check first. An excellent family museum.

Eden Craft Gallery (Penrith 67955) in the Old Grammar School, St Andrew's Churchyard, is a fairly new venture. Run by local crafts folk.

Penrith Museum (Penrith 64671) is housed in Robinson's School, Middlegate - also the home of the tourist information centre. It is a small display, and rather cramped, but nicely presented and it is free to go in.

Hutton-in-the-Forest (Skelton 500) is within striking distance of Penrith, just off the B5305, three miles north, so it seems churlish to leave it out. A mansion based around a fourteenth century pele tower. Now the home of Lord Inglewood. Nice gardens and house, but rather restricted opening times.

Just outside town, at Clifton Dykes is **Wetheriggs Country Pottery** (Penrith 62946). There's a gallery and showroom, with pottery for sale, made on site in the traditional manner. **Acorn Bank** garden, at Temple Sowerby, is an outstanding, National Trust owned herb garden. Finally, **Nunnery Walks**, at Staffield, nine miles north of Penrith (Lazonby 537) is a magnificent place to visit; lovely wooded walks beside the River Eden and some of the prettiest waterfalls in the county.

Evenings No theatre - for that you have to travel to Carlisle - but there is the **Alhambra** cinema in Middlegate (Penrith 62400).

WALKS

Walk up Wordsworth Street and you start climbing the hill which brings you to Penrith Beacon. Not a wonderful walk in itself, but worth doing for the views from the top; across the Eden valley to the fells of

Lakeland. Magnificent on a clear day. Some pleasant walks along the river at Eamont Bridge, a short distance outside town or if you'd like something more challenging, try the footpath which follows the west bank of the River Lowther to Askham.

STAYING

Handy as a base if you want to be outside the Lakes, and with the lovely Eden Valley on your doorstep, who could blame you. Very good access to the Northern Lakes, with a lot to see and do in the immediate vicinity if you want to go exploring in the car in the evening. There are a number of B&Bs and smaller guest houses. Try the **Woodland House Hotel** (Penrith 64177) in Wordsworth Street. For something grander, there's the **George Hotel** (Penrith 62696) in Devonshire Street, or, a few miles outside town, the **Edenhall Hotel** (Langwathby 454). For busy businessmen, there's the very modern **North Lakes Gateway Hotel** (Penrith 68111).

EATING

One very good restaurant, **Passepartout** (Penrith 65852), in Castlegate. Small but the menues are very imaginative. For teas and light meals, try the **Bluebell Bookshop** (Penrith 66660), Angel Square, or **In Clover** (Penrith 67474), the wholefood restaurant in Poet's Walk, the pleasant new shopping arcade.

TRANSPORT

Good bus connections with Keswick, Carlisle and, to a lesser extent, Kendal. Ribble service 24 is designed to link up with visitors arriving at Penrith station and heading for Keswick. There is also a bus service to Glenridding. The station is in Brunswick Road (Penrith 63616). Coach links to Newcastle and points east. The main line railway runs through Penrith (Penrith 62466), on route from Lancaster to Carlisle, but doesn't always stop here, so check carefully. Car parking in King Street and Middlegate, though the latter rather cramped. Also try Princes Street. Good road access to the Lakes, via the unloved A66 to Keswick, or via the A6 to Kendal. The drive up the A6, to Penrith, is attractive, as you soar over Shap. About thirty minutes to Keswick, forty-five to Kendal.

Tourist information   Robinson's School, Middlegate (Penrith 64671).

Market day   Tuesday and Saturday, early closing Wednesday.

Askham

Askham is an old established and very pretty village. It has a long, broad main street, fringed with trees and grassy banks. Someone once said to me that in Askham, the trees and the houses have equal importance in creating its character. The name means 'the place with the ash trees'. It is a Sunday afternoon sort of place. Great for rambles down muddy lanes and bridleways, or just roaming through the village. There have been a large number of cottages renovated and barns converted within the village, which helps keep the character of the place whilst maintaining a living, working community. Once in the village centre, it is easy to ignore the modern housing estate grafted onto the outskirts. A gentle, friendly village, in appearance belonging more to the Yorkshire Dales than Lakeland.

The houses are mostly mid-seventeenth and eighteenth century. At the north-west end of the village is a large, walled garden containing **Askham Hall.** This solid-looking building was fourteenth century pele tower, converted into an Elizabethan mansion in 1574 by Thomas Sandford. The Hall remained within the Sandford family until 1828, when it became the rectory. It is now the home of the Earl of Lonsdale, one of England's greatest landowners, and not open to the public.

Askham village green

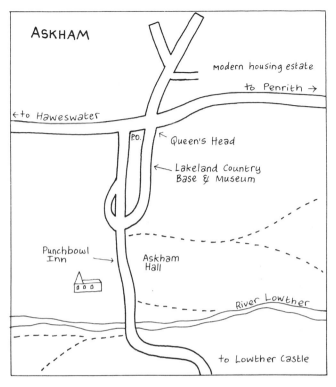

The hall stands at the lower end of the village, as the road slopes downhill towards the river. On the right, a few hundred yards past the pub, is **St Peter's Church**, a square, Victorian building in a nice position, overlooking the river.

From the centre of the village, you get glimpses of a strange, castellated structure, looming above the trees on the hillside on the far side of the river. This is **Lowther Castle**, built by architect Robert Smirke (who also built the British Museum) between 1806 and 1811. It is not a real castle; it was built as a magnificent mansion. By 1936 it was proving too expensive to maintain so the Earl of Lonsdale moved into Askham Hall. Now only the facade of the castle remains, but it is a spectacular, preudo-Gothic ruin.

Lowther Castle is within easy walking distance of Askham village; simply follow the gently winding lane over the river and up the hill through glorious English parkland. On route you will pass **St Michael's church**, an isolated building standing in a small churchyard in a commanding position, overlooking the River Lowther. Parts of the church are early thirteenth century, though the main bulk is Victorian. The strange structure in the churchyard is the Lowther Mausoleum, built in 1857. Continue along the lane, past the avenue of trees, and you come to **Lowther Newtown**, built in the 1680s by Sir John Lowther to house his estate workers.

It is very pleasant, peaceful countryside for just strolling around in. Follow the bridle way which goes behind Askham Hall, and the right of way takes you across the fields and down to the river. At the bridge, below St Peter's, turn right off the road and the wooded footpath takes you south, again along the river for most of the way. Or you can take a detour and follow the footpath past the castle - the closest the public can get to it.

For accomodation and bar meals try **The Punch Bowl** (Hackthorpe 443) or the **Queen's Head** (Hackthorpe 225).

Tourist information Pooley Bridge.

Pooley Bridge   ℂ *

The setting for Pooley Bridge is rather nicer than the village itself. It's in flat, open countryside at the foot of Lakeland's most attractive lake. The village itself consists of plain, greystone houses, a couple of hotels and a number of tourist shops. It's a bit like a miniature Coniston. The surrounding woods and the conical-shaped mound of Dunmallet Hill do give it some charm. In fact, the 'Pooley' part of its name is Norse for 'the hill with a pool'. The 'Bridge' part was not added until around 1800. Dunmallet lies just to the west of the village and is the site of an Iron Age hill fort.

Little of great architectural interest in the village. The church is a small, nineteenth century affair, lacking a churchyard. A short distance to the south is **Eusemere**, once the home of the anti-slave trade campaigner, Thomas Clarkson. It was whilst walking to visit the Clarksons, with his sister Dorothy in 1802, that Wordsworth came across the golden host of daffodils which have plagued GCSE English scholars ever since.

There are some good walks around the Pooley Bridge area. It is possible to follow a path across the fields to Dacre, returning along the River Eamont and taking in **Dalemain** on the way back. This is a fine, Georgian-fronted mansion, built around a Norman pele tower. It has been the ancestral home of the Hasell family since 1679. It's open to the public and one of the nicest stately homes in Cumbria. It has magnificent gardens, a small agricultural museum and the pele tower houses the Westmorland and Cumberland Yeomanry museum. (Further details on Pooley Bridge 450.) There's also a good walk to St Michael's church, Barton, where you can see the grave of Wordsworth's grandad.

Getting to Pooley Bridge is easy. There is a bus from Penrith or you can take a lake steamer from Glenridding (for details see Glenridding entry). By car, only fifteen minutes from Penrith, half-an-hour from Keswick, approximately three-quarters of an hour from Ambleside.

Finally, it is also worth mentioning **Sharrow Bay** (Pooley Bridge 301), one of Lakeland's premier hotels and restaurants. This stands by the lake shore, two miles south of Pooley Bridge.

Tourist information   There is a National Park information centre in Finkle Street (Pooley Bridge 530).

Dacre ℂ **

A very attractive hamlet, seldom visited by tourists despite being well within the National Park. A tidy cluster of farms and cottages, with a rather fine church, St Andrews. This quiet old building is said to be built on the site of a Saxon monastery, mentioned by the Venerable Bede in his *Ecclesiastical History*. The tower was originally Norman, but was rebuilt in the early nineteenth century. Traces remain of the original Saxon foundations. In the chancel are two parts of cross shaft, dating from the nineth or tenth century, one of which shows Adam and Eve. Out in the churchyard you will encounter four stone bears. These three-feet high curiosities mark the four corners of the original churchyard and depict a bear asleep, the bear being attacked by a wild cat, bear trying to shake the cat off, and finally bear eating the cat. Moral: If you meet any real bears, leave well alone (especially if you're a cat).

Dacre has a castle; a fourteenth century pele tower, built on the site of a much earlier structure, beside the beck. The castle has walls of seven feet thich and some rather good battlements, spoilt only by a television aerial perched on top. It is a private residence, so not open to the public.

There's a nice old pub in the village, **The Horse and Farrier** (Pooley Bridge 541). Good for pub meals, but not if you're employed by the National Park Authority; an unfriendly notice in the entrance porch reads "members of the Lake District Special Planning Board, Friends of the Earth and similar organisations are not welcome in this pub".

121

Glenridding and Patterdale

FLAVOUR

These two villages are strung along the main A592. As you descend into the valley from Kirkstone Pass, the first you encounter is Patterdale, the older of the two settlements. The name is a corruption of 'St Patrick's dale'; according to legend the patron saint of Ireland was was supposedly shipwrecked on Duddon sands in the sixth century and passed through the valley on his subsequent meanderings. There is a well dedicated to him, situated in the wall by the roadside, just before you come to the Glenridding boat landing.

Although neither village is hugely attractive in itself, both are immensely popular for their setting; in the heart of one of Lakeland's loveliest valleys, surrounded by mountains and with the serpentine splendour of Ullswater to hand. Glenridding in particular is a favourite haunt of fell walkers, providing the starting point for walks on Helvellyn, Fairfield and Place Fell. The magnificent scenery has led to a level of activity in both villages out of all proportion to their size, though it has to be said most of the transient population seems to be in the car parks, either putting on or taking off fell boots.

FACTS

Patterdale is an old farming community and the prettier of the two villages. **Patterdale Hall**, just west of the main road, mid-way between Glenridding and Patterdale, was originally seventeenth century, but rebuilt during the 1800s. It was once the home of John Mounsey, the so-called King of Patterdale.

Glenridding is a mining village. It grew up around the Greenside Mines, situated to the west, at the head of Glenridding Beck. Lead ore was first discovered here in the 1650s and commercial exploitation of the mines lasted three hundred years. The Greenside Mining Company was formed in 1822 and went on to develop the mines into a thriving, profitable enterprise, with shafts extending many hundreds of feet into the hillside. It was one of the first mining operations to utilise hydroelectric power for winding and pumping, under the management of Captain William Henry Borlase, in the 1890s. The elctric locomotive, introduced in 1892, was the first to be used in any British mine.

Until the Mining Company arrived, Glenridding was little more than a tiny hamlet. Abundant evidence of the mine workings can be found on the fellside below Hart Side, in the form of old mine buildings (the Youth Hostel is based in one of them) and the spoil tips above the

Glencoyne farm, near the shores of Ullswater. One of the finest examples of venacular architecture in the valley.

river. The last reserves of ore were mined in 1961 and the mine closed the following year.

In October 1929, the mines had a different impact on the valley when the reservoir at Kepple Cove burst one night, during heavy storms. The dam wall collapsed and over a quarter of a million gallons of water flooded into the valley, sweeping 25,000 tons of rubble into Glenridding Beck. Huge boulders were caught up the flood as it smashed down onto the village. The devestation was enormous; houses were flooded, shop counters were washed through windows, a barn and a tea room were lifted from their foundations and tons of wreckage was washed into the lake and deposited on the far shore. But although livestock perished, no one was killed. The disaster caught the local imagination and the following few days saw charabancs full of sightseers arriving at the scene. The stony peninsular used as a car park by the steamboat company is now all that remains of the disaster.

WALKS

No space to list them all here, there are just so many. For hardened fellwalkers, the route onto Helvellyn, via Striding Edge, is one of Lakeland's great classics. Helvellyn is one of Lakeland's four summits over 3000 feet high. Similarly, Fairfield and St Sunday Crag shouldn't be missed, with stupendous views of the valley and the surrounding mountains. Place Fell provides a slightly less strenuous objective, with an excellent walk to Angle Tarn which can be extended onto the summit of High Street. For low level walks, try Dovedale or along Grisedale Beck, but the favourite is the walk along the far shore of Ullswater, from Howtown to Glenridding; catch the steamer to Howtown and walk back along some of Lakeland's prettiest countryside.

Five miles north of Glenridding is another natural delight, Aira Force. Probably the Lake District's most famous waterfall. A spectacular cascade, with a nice walk up to it. There's even a car park and a cafe.

STAYING

An excellent base for the eastern fells, but a bit of a drag having to go over Kirkstone all the time to reach the Central Lakes. There are numerous B&Bs in the area, also a number of good guest houses and pubs - try the **White Lion**, Patterdale (Glenridding 214). Farther north and further upmarket is**Leeming on Ullswater**, a fine hotel on the lake shore (Pooley Bridge 444). There's also a good caravan site, **The Quiet Site**, at Watermillock (Pooley Bridge 337).

EATING

Reasonable bar meals at the **Ullswater Hotel** (Glenridding 444), excellent meals at **Leeming on Ullswater**. Nice teas at **Greystones**, a small guest house beside Glenridding Beck (Glenridding 392).

TRANSPORT

It seems rather churlish to class the Ullswater steamers as mere transport, when really they are one of the attractions of the area. They are a good way to get to and from Pooley Bridge, however, and the only practical means of getting to the start of the Howtown walk (unless you're feeling really energetic). The two steamers run throughout the summer season, with regular sailings throughout the day. Telephone the Ullswater Navigation and Transit Company, on Glenridding 229.

The only bus to make it over the Kirkstone Pass is the Moutain Goat (Windermere 5161), which runs a regular service from Ambleside and Windermere to Glenridding during the summer. Ribble run a bus service from Penrith to Glenridding (Penrith 63616).

The car journey over Kirkstone Pass is a doddle - nothing to compare to Hardknott and Wrynose. About half-an-hour to Ambleside, the same to Pooley Bridge. To get to Keswick, you can go up through Dockray and travel along the A66.

Tourist information   An attractive new National Park information centre stands in the car park at Glenridding, next to the beck. Inside there is a recreation of a mine shaft at Glenridding, which is very effective. There is a relief map of the Helvellyn range, just outside the centre, which proves very popular with walkers. Telephone Glenridding 414.

Mardale   Wet

To explore Mardale thoroughly, you will need either (a) a wet suit, aqualung, mask, snorkel and flippers, or (b) a drought. The little village of Mardale once stood at the head of the valley now occupied by Haweswater. Famed for its dairy produce, in the middle of the nineteenth century the village was sending anything up to 3,000lbs of butter a week to markets in Manchester. In 1929, the Manchester Water Corporation began building a dam, to raise the level of Haweswater. Eleven years later, the residents of Mardale were evacuated and the valley flooded.

As a result, this is usually the Lake District's quietest village. I say "usually" because in 1984 the hot summer brought about a severe drought, with the result that Mardale became visible once more. Mardale was suddenly more popular than Grasmere. Cars queued the length of the valley as people drove down the narrow lane to reach the village. Stones from the old bridge were plundered, for souvenirs. One enterprising individual even went up and down the line of traffic, selling parking tickets - until the police caught up with him. The in thing to wear that summer was a teeshirt bearing the logo "I've Seen Mardale".

Most years, the valley is quiet, secluded and placid. A good place to get away from it all. One point: if you're planning to take the plunge and investigate the village more closely, don't expect intact houses with doors open, half-eaten meals still on the tables, curtains billowing eerily with the ebb of water; all the houses were demolished before the valley was flooded.

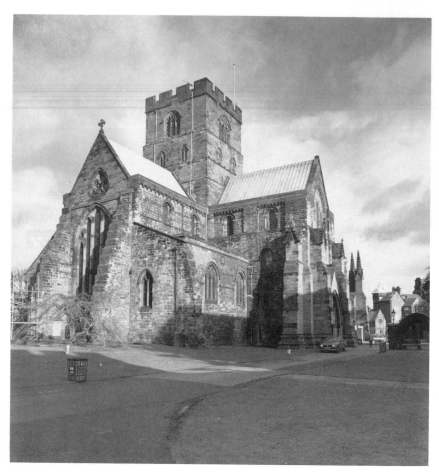

Carlisle Cathedral

Chapter 8

Carlisle

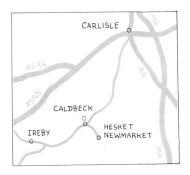

Carlisle   𝔸   **

FLAVOUR

This is it, the capital of Cumbria, the big metropolis. Not vast as cities go, but mind-bogglingly huge by Lakeland standards. You can tell which are the National Park residents out for the day, by the dazed way they stand on the pavements, staring at the traffic.

As with any city, there are parts which are seedy, ugly or just plain boring, but there are also parts which are interesting, historical and attractive. Carlisle has history practically seeping out of the brickwork. It has been built on, fought over, burnt down, beseiged, stormed and raided more times than Wordsworth saw hosts of daffodils. We are now witnessing the city during one of its quiet patches. Enjoy it before the next seige.

Most visitors come to Carlisle for the shops. It is the nearest large shopping area for those based in the north Lakes (southerners head for Lancaster). If you can't get it in Carlisle, you'll probably have to continue to Edinburgh or turn right for Newcastle. The area around the market cross has been pedestrianized, which helps matters considerably, and there is The Lanes, just across the street, a rather nice shopping arcade (but a place to avoid on Saturdays).

As the administrative capital of the county, it is busy throughout the week. To get away from the crowds, escape into Abbey Street and explore the area around the Cathedral.

You cannot mistake that you're in a Border town. Scotland feels only a step away and as you wander the streets it is hard to remember that you're still in Cumbria. If you start pining for the fells, go and savour the view from the Castle walls.

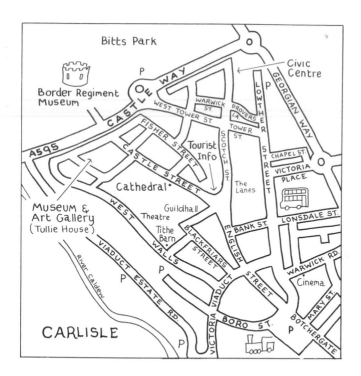

FACTS

The Romans built a town here, *Luguvalium*, to serve the garrison at Stanwix, the nearby fort on Hadrian's Wall. Roman remnents have been found during excavations, but the bulk of the first city has been built on many times subsequently.

At the time of the Norman Conquest, Carlisle was still a Saxon stronghold. (The city does not appear in the Domesday Book and it is said to be the only town in England to preserve a purely British name - *Caer-Luel*.) It was captured by William Rufus in 1092. He built a wooden castle as a permanent stronghold and maintained a garrison there. This was the beginning of the most important castle in the north-west of England, for centuries the focal point of the struggle for territory between England and Scotland. Between 1122 and 1461, it was beseiged nine times by the Scots; captured and recaptured four times. The castle was captured again during the Civil War, first by Parliamentarians (the castle fell after ten months), then by the Royalists, aqnd finally by Parliamentarians again. In 1745 it was captured by Bonnie Prince Charlie - possibly for old times sake - but recaptured for the final time shortly afterwards. It has remained in English hands ever since.

King David of Scotland first built walls round the city in 1136 but they were long and difficult to man. They enclosed an area of 45 acres, with the castle at the north-west end. Very little now remains of the walls, the expansion of the city caused the disappearance of the eastern ramparts, but the west walls survive, where expansion was limited by the River Caldew.

Henry I gave permission for the founding of a priory in the city in 1122. A church was built and in 1133 Henry I's confessor, Aethulwulf was created the first bishop of the new see. Carlisle suffered a great fire in 1292, and the cathedral and castle were extensively rebuilt. A market charter was granted in 1158.

Mary Queen of Scots was imprisoned in Carlisle Castle in 1568; she used to exercise by walking about the area below the castle's southern wall, which became known as Lady's Walk. She was held here for two months, before being sent to Bolton Castle, which was considered a far safer stronghold.

Carlisle today is the administrative capital of Cumbria. Cumbria County Council has its offices here and it is also the home of BBC Radio Cumbria and the independent Border Television.

BEST BUILDINGS

The Castle looks dour but is magnificent. It has retained its basic shape as a Norman motte and bailey castle. The oldest part of the building is the **stone keep**, built by David I of Scotland around 1150. The remainder of the castle has been rebuilt and reinforced several times over its long and troubled history. The castle houses the county archive and the Border Regiment Museum and is open to the public.

Carlisle Cathedral is smaller than most of its southern counterparts. Part of the Norman nave remains and the interior is quite beautiful. There is so much to tell and see that it requires a book in itself. The building has been rebuilt a number of times during its history but, for once, escaped being spoilt by the Victorian passion for 'improving'.

Wandering around in the vicinity of the Cathedral puts you in one of the most attractive part of Carlisle. As you leave the building, you find yourself in the **Abbey Close**. The **Deanery** was originally a sixteenth century pele tower. Head north and you pass through **Prior Slee's Gatehouse**, built in 1527, and enter **Abbey Street**, an almost unspoilt Georgian street. Nearby is **Tullie House**, built in 1689 and described by Pevsner as "the most ambitious house in Carlisle". It is Carlisle's only Jacobean building and houses the Carlisle Museum. Look out for the drainpipes, works of art in themselves.

Head back down Castle Street and you come to the centre of town, with its **market cross**, erected in 1682. At the corner of Castle Street and the pedestrianized extension of Fisher Street, is the **Guildhall**. This attractively restored building was the headquarters in the middle ages of the eight crafts guilds which formed the city corporation. The **Old Town Hall** was built in 1669 and extended in 1717. It is now the home of the tourist information centre, but at the time of writing was undergoing restoration work. (In fact, they always seem to be at it. Mostly for the best.)

There are some good eighteenth and nineteenth century buildings in **Fisher Street**. The area around English Street and Lowther Street is also nice, apart from the traffic, but Botchergate rather lets things down - best to avoid it. Carlisle must have disappointed thousands of visitors who, by mistake, turned right out of the railway station, hit the horrors of Botchergate and went straight home.

The **Railway Station** is a fascinating building, and not just for the trains. At one time, Carlisle had seven different railway companies operating from the town, a record surpassed by no other English town. Look carefully at the station building, built in 1847 by Sir William Tite; it thinks it's a Tudor palace.

Coming back to the Old Town Hall, you will have to visit the new **Lanes** shopping development. Very new and impressive, though mostly the preserve of the big chain stores, which is a pity. Don't forget the Victorian **Covered Market**. Real local produce and real local faces.

Behind Abbey Street are the only surviving remenants of the old city wall, known as **West Walls**. At the southern end is the fifteenth century **Tithe Barn**, with its splendid timber roof, restored in the nick of time.

THINGS TO DO

Carlisle is an excellent shopping centre, very busy on Saturdays. In fact, shopping seems to be the main activity of the inhabitants. Their patron saint must be St Michael. Plenty of high street multiples, plus a good range of smaller, friendlier shops. Good antiquarian and second hand bookshop. The city has a leisure centre, the recently built **Sands Centre** (Carlisle 25222).

Carlisle City Museum and Art Gallery (Carlisle 34781), also sometimes referred to as the Tullie House Museum. Good range of exhibits, including Roman remains from Hadrian's Wall. Amazing collection of pre-Raphaelite paintings. Occasional special exhibits.

Prior's Tower (Carlisle 35169) is right next to the Cathedral and houses a small museum in the pele tower. Guided tours are also available.

Border Regiment Museum (Carlisle 32774), based in Queen Mary's Tower, in the Castle.

The Old Town Hall

Evenings There is an arts theatre and gallery at Cumbria College of Art and Design, called the **Stanwix Theatre**. Holds a range of events and exhibitions throughout the year. There is the **West Walls Theatre** (Carlisle 33233). The city has two cinemas, the **Studio** (21144) and the **Lonsdale** (Carlisle 25586).

EVENTS

Carlisle Great Fair is held in late August every year. Originally established in 1353, it used to be proclaimed from the market cross at 8 a.m. on the 26th of August each year. It has been revived in recent years and now runs as a sort of mini-Edinburgh Festival.

Cumberland Show is the largest agricultural show in Cumbria. Held annually in late July.

WALKS

There are some good town trails in Carlisle, details of which can be obtained from the tourist information centre. Not so easy to escape into the countryside, though Bitts Park, to the north of the town, is very pleasant, with strolls down to the River Eden.

STAYING

Limited if you want anything high class or distinctive. The **Swallow Hilltop Hotel** (Carlisle 29255), is large and modern, while the **Cumbrian Hotel** (Carlisle 31951), smaller and nicely situated in Court Square. **The Crown and Mitre** (Carlisle 25491) used to be a posh place, but is now rather faded, but it is right in the centre, beside the Old Town Hall. Carlisle is an excellent base if you don't want to restrict yourself to the Lakes. Handy for the Borders, Hadrian's Wall, Eden Valley, the Solway and northern fells, or you could easily make a day trip to Edinburgh from here. Too far away to be useful for the southern Lakes.

EATING

Again, the choice is limited, though there is a good Italian, **Franco's** (Carlisle 34084) in Castle Street, or **Lordy's**, in Lonsdale Street (Carlisle 42014). Also a number of smaller eating places. Try **Mr Pickwick's**, in the Lanes (Carlisle 49346) - though this can get very busy - or **Hudson's** (Carlisle 47733) in Treasury Court. Finally, there's always the **Cathedral Buttery**, a very nice tearoom and bookshop, beneath the Prior's Tower.

TRANSPORT

Excellent rail links to London, Edinburgh and Scotland. Not so handy if you want to get to the Lakes; either go to Penrith and catch a bus to

Carlisle commuters hurrying to catch the rush hour trams

Town Hall and Scotch Street, Carlisle

Keswick or down to Oxenholme and take the branch line to Windermere. The railway staion is on Carlisle 44711. Buses run down to Penrith and Keswick, but the trip to Kendal is interminable. The bus station is in Lowther Street (Carlisle 21038). If you're coming by private jet, Carlisle has its own airport (Carlisle 73641). At the time of writing, public flights are limited to the Isle of Man, though Air Furness hope to operate a route to Manchester in the near future, and there is talk of an airline operating to Heathrow. 'Phone the airport for latest details.

Parking in Carlisle can be a pain, especially on Saturdays. Disc parking is in force, but parking becomes easier after 1 p.m. on Saturday afternoon, when the restriction is lifted. The best car park is between the Castle and the river. Carlisle is right next to Junction 43 on the M6. Travelling time - about ninety minutes to Windermere, via Kendal. Around forty-five minutes to Keswick.

Tourist information   Old Town Hall Carlisle 25517.

Market day   Monday to Saturday, in the covered market in Fisher Street. Early closing day on Thursday.

Ireby   ℂ   *

Like Lorton, Ireby has two centres. The main village consists of a string of houses along the road, two pubs, and a post office. It is surrounded by rolling hillside and at one time almost all the houses were farms. Just opposite the Black Lion Hotel is the remenant of a market cross. Ireby was granted a market charter in 1237 and at one time it rivalled Cockermouth. Wigton and Cockermouth proved too much competition, however. There is no longer a market, and the village has declined somewhat, though it still has a robust community feel to it. The Sun Inn (Low Ireby 346) is a nice old place which does good bar meals.

As you approach Ireby from the south, you may spot a small, whitewashed fell church across the fields, just outside the village. This stands by the road to Uldale. Dedicated to St James, it dates from 1730, though there is evidence of masonry from an earlier church, built here in 1150. Inside there is a visitors' book, begun on the 6th April 1958 and still only half full ... Between Ireby and Torpenhow is another Norman church. It now stands alone in a field, superceded by St James, built in the village in 1847.

High Ireby is even smaller; a farm and a few whitewashed cottages, situated about three-quarters of a mile to the south.

Caldbeck   B ***

FLAVOUR

The approach road to Caldbeck is over superb countryside, the wind-swept Caldbeck fells, with occasional glimpses of Skiddaw to the south. You cross a wide, rolling moor, descend into a shallow river valley and suddenly you're in Caldbeck, the Hampstead of the Northern Fells.

It is a very pretty village, with a village green and duck pond, an ancient church standing beside a charming river, a pub and a very famous resident - albeit currently residing in the churchyard. It is a moderately large, well-cared place, generally uncrowded and unhurried. You don't feel irresistably compelled to Buy Things as you wander around the village. Community life is very lively. Is this the only Lakeland village with its own squash court? There is also a thriving amateur dramatic society, a cricket club and the local Young Farmers club is the most active in all Cumbria. Perhaps the Universe.

The village has a slightly preserved air about it, a little as though it has been scrubbed clean ready for visitors. Very popular with commutors from Carlisle. On a Sunday, the pub seems to be surrounded with Volvos, Barbour jackets and Golden Retrievers.

FACTS

The village lies well away from the central fells, in the countryside beyond Skiddaw, where at one time no tourist ever ventured. If Caldbeck sneezed, it would find itself outside the National Park boundary. In fact, parts of it are already there. You can tell by the sudden outbreak of extensions and Velux windows.

A long-standing farming community, the original settlement probably grew up around the church. St Kentigern was supposed to have preached in the district during his flight from the King of Strathclyde and there is a well dedicated to him, beside the river, next to the church. This would also have been Cald Beck's main crossing point. The Prior of Carlisle built a hospice for travellers here in early medieval times. The building no longer exists, though Friar Hall Farm and Friar Row maintain a link, if only in name.

Caldbeck grew up as a rural settlement, most of the population engaged in agriculture until the discovery of mineral wealth in the Caldbeck fells. During the eighteenth century, the character of the place gradually changed, with mills built along the river to provide power. It became a thriving village, grinding corn, spinning wool, making paper, along with limestone quarrying and lead, copper and coal mining

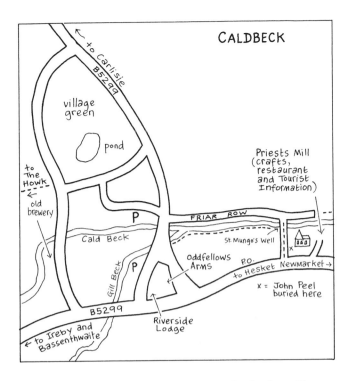

occuring in the vicinity. By 1829, there were six pubs in the village - always a sign of prosperity.

Caldbeck's most famous resident is John Peel, the huntsman with the coat so grey. Born nearby in 1777, he lived in Caldbeck and was master of the local hunt. He died in 1854 and is buried in the churchyard. The famous song was written by Woodcock Graves, who lived at Cockermouth, though the tune he used was a different one. Another celebrity now resides in the churchyard, one Mary Harrison, nee Robinson, the Beauty of Buttermere.

BEST BUILDINGS

St Kentigern's is very attractive. An early wooden church may have been erected here towards the end of the seventh century, though the earliest parts of the present building date back to the mid-1100s; part of the Norman archway still exists. The effect inside is rather grand. In the porch is part of an old cross. John Peel's grave is in the churchyard on the left.

There are a number of old mills dotted about the area, one of which, **Priests Mill**, has recently been restored. It was built in 1702 as a corn mill, and was later also used as a sawmill and joiners workshop. The waterwheel is still operating. The site of the car park used to be a tenter garth, where cloth was spread out on tenterhooks to stretch and dry. On the narrow lane behind the car park, is a substantial white cottage, looking a little out of character with its surroundings but dated 1690. Next to it is a low, brick building with a chimney. This was probably once a fulling mill, but was a **Brewery** throughout most of the nineteenth century. The main road junction stands a little distance from the village green, making the village seem rather decentralised and widespread.

THINGS TO DO

Priest's Mill (Caldbeck 369) is no longer a working mill; milling last took place here in the 1930s. Now a Grade 2 Listed Building, it has been restored in recent years and now houses a restaurant, craft workshop and small bookshop. The waterwheel and part of the mill race are still there. Attractive position, overlooking the river. There is also the **Old Smithy** craft shop, just next to the pub. And Caldbeck must be one of the few Cumbrian villages with its own Third World gift shop, opposite St Kentigern's.

WALKS

Very pleasant walking in the nearby Caldbeck Fells. Wild and isolated; you could walk all day and never meet another soul, apart, perhaps, from the occasional world-famous mountaineer. There is also a nice walk to Hesket Newmarket; follow the bridle way which extends beyond the end of Friar Row. There are pleasant strolls along the river, crossing over the packhorse bridge behind St Kentigern's (look out for the well). Or turn left out of the car park and follow the footpath sign at the road junction to head west to the amazing **Howk**. This is a wierd limestone gorge, once full of mill buildings. The original, natural stone bridge was called Fairy Bridge. Continue along the river to Whelpo and return along the road.

STAYING

Riverside Lodge (Caldbeck 234) or for B&B, **Swaledale Watch** (Caldbeck 409), just outside the village at Whelpo. The best of all is **High Greenrigg House** (Caldbeck 430), possibly the nicest guest house in the Northern Lakes and an absolute bargain. It also does good dinners for non-residents.

Joseph Strong, Caldbeck clogmaker

EATING

Try **The Oddfellow's Arms** (Caldbeck 227), now reverted to its former name, having been The John Peel Inn for a number of years. Serves the usual bar snacks. **Priest's Mill** is healthier and more attractive.

TRANSPORT

Caldbeck actually has its own coach company, though it is very small - Tyson's, on Caldbeck 237. Neat car park by the river, just below the village green, and another behind the pub. Please don't leave your car littering up the roadside.

Tourist information available at Priest's Mill.

Hesket Newmarket   C **

If few visitors get to Caldbeck, fewer still reach Hesket Newmarket. Hesket is a peaceful, unspoilt country village, with no pretentions to being a scenic tourist spot. There's a quiet main street, a village shop, a pub, a covered market cross and a strange hall. **Hesket Hall** - now somewhat ramshackle - was built in the seventeenth century for one Sir Wilfred Lawson. It has some peculiar features - notable the pyramid-shaped roof and the large, square, central chimney. The shape of the house is all angles and annexes; the story goes that it was built this way so that shadows from the twelve corners of the building contrive to act as a sundial.

Hesket was little more than a hamlet until the early eighteenth century, when a market charter was granted. The village became known as Kesket Newmarket and attracted a fair amount of trade, as well as a number of merchants who settled in the village. It never really caught on as a market town, however, and the market had closed by the end of the nineteenth century.

Charles Dickens and Wilkie Collins once passed through, on a walking tour. There is a cottage called Dicken's House directly behind the market cross.

The **Old Crown Inn** (Caldbeck 288) is a pleasant pub, popular with the locals and well-worth seeking out. Look out for one of Hesket's more famous residents, the mountaineer and writer, Chris Bonington.

Chapter 9

Furness

Ulverston

FLAVOUR

Ulverston is a friendly market town, strategically placed half-way along the Furness Peninsula. It is not the most picturesque of places but has a certain faded charm. It passed from Lancashire into Cumbria with local government disorganisation in 1974 and it retains a down-to-earth Northern flavour which has more in common with Preston and Lancaster than the Lakes.

The town really comes into its own on market day. Ulverston has one of the best markets in Cumbria; lively, busy, interesting, with a long history and no concessions to the tourist industry. It is primarily an agricultural market, where farmers gather to trade, but there are more general stalls crowding the pavements in Market Square and extending into New Market Street and Brogden Street.

When the market is missing, the town looks rather sorry for itself. Despite attempts by a few individuals to attract more visitors to the town, it never seems to try very hard, compared to that other non-National Park market town, Cockermouth. This is a shame as the place has just as much potential as a tiny Lakeland town such as Hawkshead.

FACTS

Ulverston's market charter was granted by Edward I in 1280. The charter gave permission for a market to be held every Thursday, with a Fair in September. The market continues on Thursdays, with a smaller market in the streets on Saturdays, and the Fair was revived in 1980 as a Charter Festival.

Ulverston enjoyed early prosperity as part of the iron industry run by the monks of Furness Abbey. Abundant natural resources throughout the area and close links with the sea made it one of the most important towns in southern Cumbria. In the late eighteenth and early

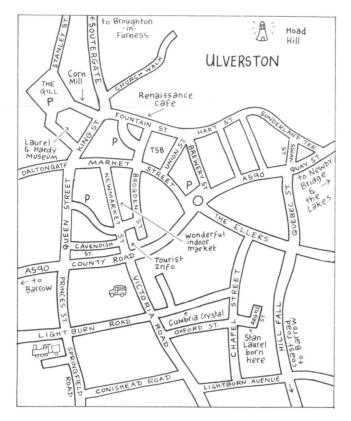

nineteenth centuries, Ulverston became a boom town, with extensive industry and trade. In 1774 there were around 70 ships operating from the area around Bardsea. In 1795, the great engineer John Rennie built a mile-long canal to link Ulverston with the sea, making Ulverston the capital of Furness. Over a thousand ships used the canal in 1828. Using my favourite indicator of industrial prosperity, in 1850 there were fifty-eight inns and three breweries in the town. There are now somewhat fewer pubs, but there's still a brewery, Hartley's, in Brewery Street.

The Furness Railway arrived in 1846, largely rendering the canal obsolete. The canal was allowed to silt up and the centre of trade and industry shifted to Barrow, causing Ulverston to slip into a gentle decline. It has recovered some of its old vigour since the war and is now the base for Glaxo's and a number of light engineering industries.

Swarthmoor Hall was regularly visited by George Fox, who made it the headquarters of the Society of Friends. On 16 June, 1890, Stanley Jefferson was born at 3 Argyle Street. He later went to America, teamed up with Oliver Hardy and, as Stan Laurel, became one of the twentieth century's greatest comedians. .

140

BEST BUILDINGS

The cobbled **Market Square** with its cross is very attractive, although the cross is actually a war memorial. The original cross was removed in 1822 and this replacement designed along the lines of a medieval market cross by W.G.Collingwood. The Square slopes down into Market Street and at the corner with Union Street is the **TSB Savings Bank**, described by Pevsner as "the best building in town". A very Italianate design, it was built in1838 by George Webster. The ornate clock tower was added eight years later. Opposite, in Brogden Street, is a rather grand **Co Op** building, built in 1881. There are some nice alleys and side streets which repay a good aimless wander around.

One or two shop fronts could do with tidying up and there have been a few modern buildings grafted unceremoniously onto the older shops and houses. The Walter Wilson Supermarket in King Street is a particularly ugly example. The architect must have based it on Lego. It was with foreboding and gloom that I learnt recently of a their proposed new supermarket in The Gill. I also have severe doubts about the flash new hotel development on the corner of Market and New Market Streets. The town needs some money spent on it, but it needs to be done with care and attention. It would be a great pity if the streets were spoilt by grotesque glass-front superstores. Ulverston has so far remembered the importance of corner shops and local stores, yet I can't help wondering how long it will last.

Ulverston auction market

141

Packing away the soapbox and returning to the buildings, the **railway station** is over a hundred years old and a fine example of railway architecture, though now very ramshackle. The parish church, **St Mary's**, is largely Victorian, but there was a church here in 1111 A.D. Traces of the original building can be found in the Norman south door. The tower was constructed in the sixteenth century and survived the attentions of the Victorian 'improvers'. Originally there was a steeple, but it was destroyed in a storm.

In Mill Street there is a careful restoration of a seventeenth century **Corn Mill**. Now open as a craft shop and gallery, the water wheel and machinery have been restored. Go outside and look carefully at the corner of the building nearest King Street - a couple of feet above the pavement you will find a curious stone carving of a series of heads.

As you approach the town by road from the north, you can't miss the **Barrow Monument** on Hoad Hill. This hundred foot high replica of the Eddystone Lighthouse was erected in 1850 as a monument to Sir John Barrow. Born in Ulverston in 1764, he was a writer, traveller, Arctic explorer and for forty years, Secretary of the Admiralty.

Just a short distance from town, on Priory Road, is **Conishead Priory**. Nothing remains of the original priory, the present building was constructed around 1823 as a Gothic mansion for Colonel R G Braddyll (he also built a set of pseudo-classical ruins on nearby Chapel Island, to give his view a more picturesque air). It was renowned as a showplace in the nineteenth century, with 200 acres of beautiful grounds. It is now owned and run by the Manjushri Institute, a community of Buddhist monks.

THINGS TO DO

The Laurel and Hardy Museum, Upper Brook Street (Ulverston 52292), is an eccentric little enterprise. In reality, it is one man's shrine to the great comedian, set up and run by Son of the Desert and ex-Mayor of Ulverston, Bill Cubin. He claims to have the world's largest collection of Laurel and Hardy memorabilia. It's good to see that someone is trying to preserve a little bit of Ulverston's history.

Ulverston Point is a good craft gallery, set in the old Corn Mill in Mill Street (Ulverston 56162). On Lightburn Road is **Cumbria Crystal** (Ulverston 54400), on of the North's premier glass manufacturers. Rumours exist that it may be moving soon to a new site at Canal Head.

Conishead Priory (Ulverston 54029) has been restored and opened. In addition to a little Buddhist soft sell, you can experience the grounds and tour the house.

Evenings **The Renaissance Theatre Trust** (Ulverston 52299), Fountain Street, organises a wide range of shows and events, bringing touring theatre and music groups into the area from all over the country. Smaller events and talks are held in their own premises, larger events in the Coronation Hall. Ulverston's cinema is **The Roxy** (Ulverston 52340) in Brogden Street. Cinema

EVENTS

The **Charter Festival** is held for a week each year, during the week containing the 11th September. Details from the tourist information centre. **Market day** is an event in itself; Thursday is better than Saturday.

WALKS

Good walk from the town centre to the Barrow Monument. Follow Hart Street to Hoad Lane and follow the path up the hill. Magnificent all round views.

STAYING

A good base, well out of the tourist crowds, though it does mean you've a half-hour trek every morning before you start getting back into the Lakes. You're not confined to the A592, however. You have the choice of several routes to the fells; either straight up to Bowness; through the Rusland Valley to Satterthwaite and Hawkshead; via Blawith to Coniston; or through Lowick Bridge to reach the Duddon Valley and points west. Try **The Virginia House Hotel** (Ulverston 54844) on Queen Street.

EATING

Good cafe at the **Renaissance Theatre Trust**. Two good and comparatively new restaurants, **The Pepper Mill** (Ulverston 57564) in Market Street, and **The Bay Horse** (Ulverston 53972) at Canal Foot.

TRANSPORT

Good bus links to Barrow, Coniston and Newby Bridge, with connections from the latter to Grange, Kendal and Windermere. The railway is on the Furness Line, between Lancaster and Barrow. Car parking on the streets is restricted, but there are a number of good car parks which,

143

at the time of writing, are free! Long may that continue. The car park in The Gill is the best and very handy for town. Traffic is not a huge problem in Ulverston, especially now the by-pass has been arranged. Allow a good forty minutes to reach Windermere and Bowness, about the same to Grange and twenty minutes to Barrow.

Tourist information   Coronation Hall (Ulverston 57120).

Market days Thursday and Saturday - of which Thursday's is the best; more market stalls and the auction market is in progress. Don't forget the indoor market in Newmarket Street, which is open throughout the week, except early closing day. Early closing Wednesday.

Grange-over-Sands   𝔹 **

FLAVOUR

Grange is a grey, limestone town, perched on the steep, wooded hillside overlooking Morcambe Bay. Over the years it has promoted itself in a number of ways, perhaps the oddest being as "Cumbria's Riviera" (oh that it was), complete with a shot of the solitary palm tree, by the station.

The place has long had a reputation for its mild climate and gentle scenery, making it more attractive to an older age group than, say, Bowness. It has grown into a retirement town, though one wonders why occasionally as you toil up Fell Road ...

The promenade is Grange's most popular feature. A gentle and relaxing place to stroll on a summer's afternoon, or better still, a warm evening in September, when you can look across the bay at Morcambe illuminations. The railway cuts across the Bay within a few feet of high tide, shutting in the town and making the muddy beach rather inaccessible. This has prevented the town from becoming a Cumbrian Blackpool. You rarely see bathers here, only the occasional intrepid windsurfer.

There are a number of very pleasant parks, the best being the Ornamental Gardens, beside the railway station. This attracts a wide variety of wildlife and is very popular with residents and visitors alike. In fact, the whole area is a rich hunting ground for naturalists. The Nature Conservancy Council runs the Merlewood research station, situated between Grange and Lindale.

Grange is a difficult place to sum up. If you live here, it can be dead boring, with little provision for youngsters. To the visitor, though, its

The Ornamental Gardens

gentility, mild climate and beautiful scenery have combined to make it the most successful of the Cumbrian seaside resorts.

FACTS

Cartmel Priory maintained a 'grange' here - from which it gets its name. They kept a vinyard and ran a small harbour. There was a small quay, below the area now occupied by the Grange Hotel. Sea coal was landed

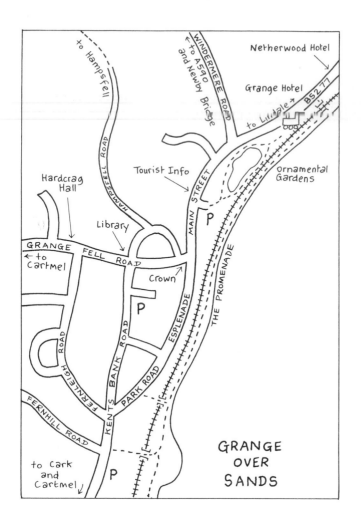

here and taken by road to the Priory.

　　With the decline of the Priory, Grange sank back to become a tiny hamlet. Its fortunes were restored in 1857 with the arrival of the railway. The town's reputation for moderate temperatures and the beauty of its surroundings made it a popular resort and it gradually became a fashionable Victorian watering place. Waters from Holy Well at Humphrey Head were famed as a remedy for "stone, gout and cutaneous complaints". A number of hotels were built and in 1904 the promenade was opened. During the last half of the nineteenth century, Grange grew from a hamlet of 70 houses and 260 inhabitants, to a town with a population of nearly 1800.

BEST BUILDINGS

The buildings are mostly Victorian, quite pleasant to look at but nothing of great antiquity. The **Netherwood Hotel** has rather a fine outlook, with serried rows of hedges. It was built in 1893 as a private house. The Grange Hotel nearby is older, 1866, but the **Crown Hotel** was probably first, built on the hill overlooking the Bay in the early nineteenth century.

The location of the early 'grange' may have been somewhere in the region of Yewbarrow Lodge. The name was applied to a farm in the early nineteenth century, which stood on the site of the present police station.

At Humphrey Head there is a farm which incorporates a pele tower. This is **Raisholme Tower**, one of a string built along the Cumbrian coast to ward of the Scots.

THINGS TO DO

Some nice shops and pleasant cafes. **Holker Hall** (Flookburgh 328) is an outstanding stately home and well-worth visiting, only a few miles away, just the other side of Cark-in-Cartmel. There is an open air swimming pool on the sea front, just west of the Esplenade.

WALKS

The route from Lancaster to Furness used to lie across Morcambe Bay, from Hest Bank to Kents Bank, two miles south of Grange. It is still an official highway, with a guide appointed by the Duchy of Lancaster. Trips across the Bay are organised every year and this is a walk which should not be missed. *Warning:* on no account should you attempt this walk without a guide - Morcambe Bay has notorious quicksands which make crossing unaccompanied extremely dangerous.

One walk you can do on your own, is up Humphrey Head, three miles to the south. This limestone headland gives superb views across the Bay to Morcambe. The last wolf in England was supposedly killed here - a likely tale. Presumably it had come to Grange to retire. As a reward, its slayer is said to have been rewarded by being allowed to marry the daughter of Raisholme Tower.

Another excellent walk begins in Windermere Road and takes you onto Hampsfell (see Cartmel), with more good views and a route down into Cartmel village.

STAYING

A number of fine hotels, some with excellent views. Try **The Grange Hotel** (Grange-over-Sands 3666) or **The Netherwood** (Grange-over-Sands 2552). Smaller and perhaps more characterful is **Hardcragg Hall** (Grange-over-Sands 3353) on Grange Fell Road. Grange is a good base to explore the southern Lakes, but rather inconvenient for the north. A good bet for accomodation if you have arrived late on a bank holiday without booking in advance (tut, tut) and the rest of the Lakes is booked solid.

EATING

Good restaurant and bar meals at the **Netherwood** and **Hardcragg Hall**. Also try the **Crown Hotel** (Grange-over-Sands 3073). Excellent cafe, **At Home** (Grange-over-Sands 4400) on Main Road. Good pub meals at **The Lindale Inn** (Grange-over-Sands 2416), two miles outside the town, in Lindale village.

TRANSPORT

There are good railway and bus links from Grange, to Lancaster and Barrow by train or to Kendal, Newby Bridge and Ulverston by bus. Change at Newby Bridge for Windermere. Car parking in town can be awkward, with restricted parking. Use the car parks in Main Street and Kents Bank Road.

Tourist information   Victoria Hall, Main Street. Grange-over-Sands 4026.

Cartmel   𝔹 ***

FLAVOUR

A lovely little village with a beautiful square, complete with market cross, waterpump and trough, though now disfigured by the recent addition of a concrete litter bin - a prime example of municipal vandalism.

    A very quiet village during the week, much easier to explore than Hawkshead and in some ways far more attractive. It hasn't sold itself to commercialism yet and doesn't have the feeling of an open air museum that is so strong in Hawkshead. The River Eea is very pretty,

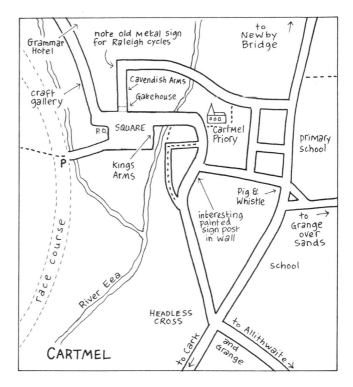

especially from the bridge as you enter the square, and Cartmel Priory is magnificent from all angles, but probably most impressive seen from across the fields.

Cartmel is a very popular village at Sunday lunchtimes, owing to the presence of several good pubs, though this usually means that the square is overrun with parked cars.

The village has not been spoilt by becoming too popular. It is still a community and is saved from becoming too twee or olde worlde by its lively character.

FACTS

The parish of Cartmel covers an area much larger than the village itself, taking in the neighbouring villages of Cark, Flookburgh and Allith-waite, as well as Grange-over-Sands and a huge tract of land stretching between the Leven and Kent estuaries and extending to Winster and Windermere. In very early days, there was no village as such, merely a scattering of tiny hamlets and settlements, distributed throughout the parish. It is only in recent times that the name has come to mean the village alone - until well into the nineteenth century it was still known

Cartmel Priory

as 'Cartmel Churchtown'.

Sometime between 670 and 685 A.D. Egfrith, the King of Northumberland, granted Cartmel and everyone in it to St Cuthbert, the great bishop of Lindisfarne. The Anglians built a chapel in the area, probably at Allithwaite. When the Normans arrived the village of Cartmel didn't exist. This area was still a stretch of marshy ground between the River Eea and Mere Beck.

In 1185 King John gave the area to William Marshall, one of the most respected nobles of his day. He became Earl of Pembroke in 1189 and the same year founded a priory for the Canons Regular of St Augustine. A chapel was built here and the influence of the so called 'black canons' spread extensively. In 1280, they were licensed by the king to import goods from Ireland and built the tiny harbour at Grange.

The original Priory underwent a number of changes over the centuries. The gatehouse was added around 1340, prompted by Scottish raids in the region. At the same time, the chapel was ordered rebuilt by Lord John Harrington. Restoration and reconstruction occured in the fifteenth, seventeenth and nineteenth centuries. It survived Henry

VIII's Dissolution of the Monastries because the locals hit on the wheeze of claiming that it was the parish church, as well as a priory. The building fared less well when a bunch of Cromwellian soldiers camped in it for the night in 1643. In addition to smashing up the organ and some of the furnishings, they also peppered one of the doors with bullets.

BEST BUILDINGS

The **Priory** remains an outstandingly beautiful building, though only the gatehouse and part of the chapel remain of the original Norman church. The interior of the building is very calm and stately. The great east window has survived largely intact since it was installed around 1425. It was inspired by the windows of York Minster. Part of the original medieval glasswork is now in St Martin's Church, Bowness. There are some beautiful misericords, amazingly intact. In the chapel, there is a tomb to Lord Harrington and his wife, dating from 1347. There is far more to see than can be covered here but, on a final note, go to the small nail-studded door at the entrance to the south-west aisle and look for the bullet holes.

There are some nice houses in the lanes leading off from the square (note the doctor's surgery and the alarming medicine bottles displayed in the window) and there is a wonderful example of an old village corner shop (except that it's not on a corner), **Bridge Stores**, as you enter the square.

THINGS TO DO

One or two nice shops, a good second-hand bookshop in the Square (Peter Bain Smith, Cartmel 369), art gallery in the National Trust-owned Priory Gatehouse, plus one or two smaller, privately-run galleries of a crafty nature.

EVENTS

Cartmel Show - excellent arts and agricultural show held Wednesday after first Monday in August; **Cartmel Races** - famous (and smallest) National Hunt course with racing held Spring and Late Summer bank holidays (Sunday and Mondays), well-worth visiting for the atmosphere alone, with refreshment tents and often a small fairground in addition to the racing.

WALKS

There is a good walk from Cartmel to Grange-over-Sands, via Hampsfell, the massive limestone escarpment to the east of the village. Excellent views of the whole valley. At the top is a limestone hospice, looking a bit like a Neolithic bus shelter. From the direction finder on its roof you can see everything from Blackpool Tower to Skiddaw ...

STAYING

A good choice if you want to be out of the crowds of Lakeland, though it does make it rather a trek to get up to Keswick. But lots to explore locally. Not a lot of B&B. One or two good hotels. **Uplands**, Haggs Lane (Cartmel 248), a very pleasant, upmarket hotel, modelled after Miller Howe, but at half the price. Run by two of John Tovey's former right-hand persons. The **Grammar Hotel** (Cartmel 367), is a small country house hotel on the outskirts of the village, with views over the race track (could be a good bet for race days if you get the right bedroom).

Cartmel's unique painted signpost , dating from the days when the route over Morecambe Bay and the Levens Estuary was a major highway. (See the map for its location.)

EATING

Plenty of pubs to choose from; try the **Cavendish Arms** (Cartmel 240), just round the corner from the square. **Uplands** also very good, though at the other end of the price scale. Some nice cafes, try **St Mary's Lodge** (Cartmel 379), by the Priory.

TRANSPORT

Bus links to Grange (connections to Kendal) and Newby Bridge (Windermere, Ulverston). Cartmel has a train station - well, almost. It's down at Cark. Part of the Lancaster to Barrow line, change at Lancaster for the main line to Carlisle and Crewe.

A car is necessary if you seriously intend to explore the Lakes, otherwise it could take an age. About 50 minutes to the M6 (junction 36, or 35 at Carnforth). Cars and Cartmel don't really mix, it spoils the view. Good car park through the Square, by the race track, so you've no excuse for parking in the Square itself. The village gets very crowded on Race days, so get there early.

Tourist information Grange-over-Sands.

Appendix

Opinions

Just to be nosey, we asked a few people connected with Lakeland to tell us how they feel about the towns and villages, to choose their favourite places, and anything they don't like:

Chris Bonington
Mountaineer, author and broadcaster

Towns: "I must give modern Carlisle an accolade. Some of the developments there have been super. The Lanes is very tastefully done, one of the nicest shopping centres I've seen in Britain. Whitehaven is extraordinarily attractive in a sad, battered way. If you're driving down that bypass road with the sunset ahead of you the harbour can look really very attractive. And there is some superb Georgian architecture."

Villages: "Just to be parochial, Caldbeck. It's a very special, super, dynamic village. It's got a squash club, a cricket club, amateur dramatics. It's a real, live, living village. It's my favourite. Hesket [Newmarket] is Caldbeck's quiet cousin. It's got one of the best pubs in the Lake District, the Crown. A really nice, friendly atmosphere."

Buildings: "It's a very subjective thing, but I've got a soft spot for the west coast mining villages, because we lived there for a time. Villages like Kirkland are unpretentious, with rows of attractive, painted houses. Not beautiful or pretty, pretty, but not too touristy like Hawkshead."

Dislikes: "The biggest eyesore in Cumbria is Carlisle Civic Centre. It's a big, high-rise block which just sticks up and can be seen for miles around."

Melvyn Bragg
Broadcaster and writer

Towns: "I've got to put Wigton first, haven't I [his birthplace], but I do like it, I think it's a smashing town. I enjoy plain towns and plain villages. Then Cartmel, for the Priory, the square and the racecourse. They're all so unexpected, like an Italian town. Thirdly, Cockermouth. It's a handsome town, with a handsome main street and some grand Georgian buildings."

Villages: "Ireby, of course [his present Lakeland home], as a plain village. After that, Lorton and then Troutbeck, for Townend."

Buildings: "I'm very fond of that line of big Victorian hotels up on the hill in Windermere, near the station. I like the great sweep of them. In Keswick, I like the jumble of alleys in the centre, but only in the winter. Keswick is best in the winter. You can't see anything in the summer. Tullie House in Carlisle is terrific, and all the buildings round the Cathedral and in Fisher Street. I'm very fond of the string of houses under Skiddaw at Applethwaite."

Dislikes: "The roundabout outside Keswick. What a way for people to enter the Lake District."

A postcard of a pub we DON'T recommend visiting - The Dun Bull, Mardale

Hunter Davies
Writer, broadcaster, and sometimes publisher

Towns: "Carlisle. No, not just 'cos it's my home town, but because I honestly think it's the most improved town in Cumbria, perhaps all Britain. The changes in the last twenty years have almost all been for the better, and you can't say that about many places. Walking around the Cathedral, through the back lanes, along Fisher Street and Abbey Street, to the Old Town Hall is now brilliant. I do get upset when South Cumbrians say they hate Carlisle. It's not Barrow you know.

"Cockermouth is even nicer, as it's smaller and you can park. They never had a stage of civic rebuilding, so little has been ruined. I love standing in Main Street, looking above the shop fronts and wondering at how little has changed. Also Kirkgate, which is knockout.

"Of the Lakeland towns proper, then it's got to be Hawkshead, the prettiest town in all Cumbria, no question. It is a bit sort of Cotswoldy, olde English tourist trap, but I love it all the same. I can't get the hang of Windermere and Bowness. I can never find the middle."

Villages: "The prettiest is probably Maulds Meaburn, saved from the hordes by being over in the Eden Valley. Watendlath in the Lakes proper is marvellous, what a setting. And I've always liked Hesket Newmarket for that row of houses either side, each one slightly different."

Buildings: "I wouldn't mind Mirehouse for my country pad, not too enormous, lovely situation, even though Bass Lake is the most boring of the lakes. Sharrow Bay for the view, though the house is very ordinary. Nab Cottage as a small place is very attractive, right on Rydal Water. Pity about the traffic."

Dislikes: "Keswick, Ambleside, Windermere and Bowness in the summer. That modern row of junk housing at Chapel Stile. Ugh."

Cressida Pemberton-Pigott
Photographer

Towns: "I think it's Keswick, because I've grown up with it, but I must say that they've done quite a lot of damage to it within the last twenty years. They've spoilt it quite a lot."

Villages: "Hesket Newmarket. You come over the hill and see it and it's so lovely and untouched."

Best buildings: "Ormathwaite Hall, at Skiddaw. Its attractive and surprising, with lovely diamond paned windows."

Dislikes: "Tarn Howes. It reminds me of Surrey."

Brian Redhead
Broadcaster, president of the Council for National Parks

Towns: "I have to put Penrith first as I was evacuated there for four years during the war. I still love it. I get a lump in my throat every time I get near it. Then Cockermouth. I do seem to prefer towns on the fringes. With Cockermouth, you don't feel its character has been destroyed by tourism. Strictly amongst the Lake District towns, then I think I have to choose Hawkshead. I have spent a lot of time in Ambleside, and I like it, but I feel Hawkshead is a special place, despite the car park. The shape has not been destroyed. I like the way the stone is cut. In Ambleside, it's nineteenth century stone and they cut it almost like brick. In Hawkshead, it's eighteenth century and they cut it bigger, so it looks like stone and is much nicer, I think."

Villages: "I have a great affection for Patterdale. I spent a lot of time there when we used to have a weekend cottage at Grasthwaitehow. I also like Hartsop, for the spinning galleries. And Dockray."

Buildings: "Dalemain, that's a great favourite. You always get a good view of it when you drive past, and I always think if I was very rich, I'd like to live there. But I suppose, hold on, of all the buildings, Hawkshead Grammar School is my favourite. It's so exactly as you'd expect Wordsworth's school to be. You can believe he went there. I just love taking people to see it."

Dislikes: "The timeshare in Langdale. Yes I know you can't see much of it from the road, but I dislike all the timeshare complexes in Lakeland. I don't like anything I don't believe in."

Dr William Rollinson
lecturer and author

Towns: "Ulverston. A typical, lively Cumbrian market town, especially on Thursdays. Some interesting architecture, including the old Town Mill, now a gift shop and coffee room. An oustanding delecatessan - where else in Cumbria can you buy sheep milk cheese, Norwegian goat milk cheese *and* Waberthwaite Cumberland sausage? Two excellent eating places - the small, friendly and unpretentious Pepper Mill Restaurant and the new gourmet restaurant, The Bay Horse, overlooking Morecambe Bay."

Villages: "Cartmel. Two outstanding medieval buildings, the Gatehouse and the Priory, which seems to ride over the village like a galleon at anchor. Several good pubs providing bar snacks, and a splendid antiquarian bookshop."

Best buildings: "Cartmel Fell Church. Tucked away in the fells, this is a little-known gem. Fifteenth century painted glass, originally from Cartmel Priory, box pews, one with traces of medieval painting. Arrow-sharpening marks not only on the porch but on the surrounding rocks."

Dislikes: "The underpass near the roundabout in Keswick - totally out of place. And, worst of all, the waterski school at the Lowwood Hotel - Stalag-on-Windermere. This is an abomination and destroys what was once one of the finest views across Windermere to the Langdale Pikes."

Richard Vane
chairman of the National Park's Development Control Committee, son of Lord Inglewood

Towns: "Appleby, because most visitors to Cumbria tend not to think it worth a visit. It's a terrific place."

Villages: "Hartsop. I can't think of any particular reason for this. Just go and look at it."

Best buildings: "Hutton-in-the-Forest [his home]. I'd be a fool to spend so much time, effort and money on it otherwise."

Dislikes: "The Herbies [revolting giant plastic trees for kiddies to play in - *Ed*] outside the Ullswater Hotel. Not because they are intended as two fingers at the Development Control Committee, but because they've upset so many people."

John Wyatt
Author, ex-National Park chief ranger

Towns: "I have to quote the old adage – 'God made the country, Man made the town and the Devil made the country town'. I've no favourite town, but to shop in I would choose those where I would expect curteous and efficient service - Grange-over-Sands, Ulverston and Egremont. Visually, Broughton-in-Furness is the least spoiled. I've everyone else's hatred of Bowness in the crowded season, but let's give full marks to the council workmen who maintain the great display of flowers along the lake front."

Villages: "I don't like any of them. They don't compare well with the villages of the Dales or Yorkshire Moors, or those of the Eden Valley. They're spoiled."

Best building: "Mirehouse at Bassenthwaite. It hasn't been expanded in an ugly way like some of them."

Dislikes: "The Aquarius building at Bowness. It might have won an architectural prize but it doesn't get one from me. I'd sooner have the corrugated iron sheds which used to stand there."

The Best Kept Village Competition

This is a competition which has been run in Cumbria for over thirty years. The villages are judged more for neatness and tidyness than for architectural merit, and covers the whole county, rather than just the Lakes, but it is a useful pointer to places worth seeking out. Over the past few years, the winners have been:

	Best kept large village	Best kept small village
1980	Morland	Ravenstonedale
1981	Dalston	Underbarrow
1982	Braithwaite	Ireby
1983	Braithwaite	Warcop
1984	Lazonby	Bassenthwaite
1985	Grasmere	Bouth
1986	Dalston (nr. Carlisle)	Great Salkeld (Penrith)
1987	Natland (nr. Kendal)	Wreay (nr. Carlisle)

Finally ...okay, we give in - here's a postcard of views from our favourite town in all Cumbria ...